It's Your
World,
So Change It

Tom Head

D1565790

800 East 96th Street, Indianapolis, Indiana 46240 USA

ISBN-13: 978-0-7897-3977-3

ISBN-10: 0-7897-3977-1

Library of Congress Cataloging-in-Publication Data

Head, Tom.

It's your world, so change it : using the power of the Internet to create social change / Tom Head.

p. cm.

ISBN 978-0-7897-3977-3

1. Internet--Social aspects. 2. Internet--Political aspects. 3. Online social networks--Political aspects. 4. Social change. 5. Social action. I. Title.

HM851.H427 2010

303.48'40285--dc22

2010020808

Printed in the United States of America

First Printing: June 2010

Trademarks

Warning and Disclaimer

Bulk Sales

Que Publishing offers excellent discounts on this book when ordered in quantity for bulk purchases or special sales. For more information, please contact

U.S. Corporate and Government Sales
1-800-382-3419
corpsales@pearsontechgroup.com

For sales outside of the U.S., please contact

International Sales
international@pearson.com

Associate Publisher
Greg Wiegand

Acquisitions Editor
Rick Kughen

Development Editor
Rick Kughen

Managing Editor
Patrick Kanouse

Project Editor
Mandie Frank

Copy Editor
Barbara Hacha

Indexer
Tim Wright

Proofreader
Language Logistics, LLC

Technical Editor
Melody Drnach

Publishing Coordinator
Cindy Teeters

Designer
Anne Jones

Compositor
TnT Design, Inc.

Reviewers
Melody Drnach
Sandi Lyman
Liz Newbury

Contents at a Glance

	Introduction	1
Chapter 1:	Online Activism 101	5
Chapter 2:	How to Research Issues and Stay Informed	13
Chapter 3:	How to Plan, Promote, and Maintain a Website	23
Chapter 4:	Engage with Social Networking Sites	43
Chapter 5:	A Short Guide to the Ethics and Etiquette of Online Activism	51
Chapter 6:	How to Raise Funds Online	63
Chapter 7:	How to Use Multimedia as an Activism Tool	73
Chapter 8:	How to Keep Allies and Supporters in the Loop	89
Chapter 9:	Action Alerts and Online Petitions	103
Chapter 10:	It's Your World, So Change It	113
Appendix A:	The 10 Common Online Activism Mistakes and How to Fix Them	127
Appendix B:	Online Activism Careers and Volunteer Opportunities	133
Appendix C:	A Short History of Online Activism Technologies	139
Appendix D:	Glossary of Terms	157
Appendix E:	Online Degree Programs for Activists	167

Table of Contents

Introduction 1

1   **Online Activism 101** **5**

A New Tool, Not a New Project 7

Where Do I Begin? 8

    Branching Out 8

    Planting Seeds 10

2   **How to Research Issues and Stay Informed** **13**

General Resources 15

Print Publications 17

Laws and Legislation 18

Keeping Up with News Sites and Blogs 19

Your E-Activism Toolkit: Getting Informed 21

3   **How to Plan, Promote, and Maintain a Website** **23**

Finding Your Audience 24

    Organizing Local Supporters 24

    Nonlocal Supporters 29

    Making Your Website Media Friendly 35

Being Found 38

    Search Engines 38

    Cross-Links 39

    Repeat Visitors 39

    Social Networking 39

    Print 40

    Word of Mouth 40

    Five Steps to Building a Great Activism Website 40

Your E-Activism Toolkit: Building a Website 41

4   **Engage with Social Networking Sites** **43**

Social Networking 101 44

    Facebook 46

    MySpace 48

    Other Social Networking Sites 48

Summary: Social Networking 49

5   **A Short Guide to the Ethics and Etiquette**
    of Online Activism **51**

    Deadly Sin #1: Self-Promotion at the Expense of the Movement ..53

    Deadly Sin #2: Unsolicited Bulk Email 54

    Deadly Sin #3: Hacktivism 55

Deadly Sin #4: Violating Copyright 57
Deadly Sin #5: Nagging 57
Deadly Sin #6: Violating Privacy 58
Deadly Sin #7: Being Scary 59
Your E-Activism Toolkit: Following the Rules 61

6   How to Raise Funds Online **63**
Other Ways to Raise Funds 68
Processing Online Donations 69
Your E-Activism Toolkit: Raising Money 71

7   How to Use Multimedia as an Activism Tool **73**
Online Multimedia Content That Changed the World 74
The Iranian Protests of 2009 75
The Burmese Protests of 2007 76
Abu Ghraib 77
Justice for Oscar Grant 78
"Macaque" 79
The 2006 May Day Protests in MacArthur Park 80
Online Video and How to Stream It 80
Finding Photographs You Can Use 82
The Art of Podcasting 83
Great Podcasts for Activists 84
Your E-Activism Toolkit: Using Multimedia 87

8   How to Keep Allies and Supporters in the Loop **89**
Not Necessarily the Newsletter 91
Using Twitter 93
Blogging 98
Your E-Activism Toolkit: Keeping Allies in the Loop 101

9   Action Alerts and Online Petitions **103**
Writing Effective Action Alerts 104
Are Massive Online Petitions a Waste of Time? 108
Your E-Activism Toolkit: Action Alerts and Petitions 111

10   It's Your World, So Change It **113**
Four Offline Technologies That Changed Activism 115
The Printing Press 115
The Telephone 117
The Radio 118
Television 120

Four Online Activism Technologies That Are Still Catching On 121
  Collaborative Documents 122
  Mobile Access 122
  Integration of Web 2.0 Proprietary Standards 122
  Security 123
Your E-Activism Toolkit: Putting It All Together 123
  Concerned Citizen 123
  Professional Online Activists 124
  Outreacher 125

A   **The 10 Common Online Activism Mistakes
    and How to Fix Them** **127**
B   **Online Activism Careers and Volunteer Opportunities** ...**133**
C   **A Short History of Online Activism Technologies** **139**
D   **Glossary of Terms** **157**
E   **Online Degree Programs for Activists** **167**

About the Author

Tom Head is author or coauthor of 24 nonfiction books on a wide range of topics, including *Civil Liberties: A Beginner's Guide* (Oneworld, 2009) and *Get Your IT Degree and Get Ahead* (Osborne/McGraw-Hill, 2000). He covers civil liberties for About.com, a division of The New York Times Company with 34 million unique visitors per month, and also blogs on civil liberties issues in his home state of Mississippi via the Mississippi Human Rights Report. He also serves as an elected trustee for the Mississippi ACLU, as VP/policy of the Mississippi branch of the National Organization for Women (NOW), as communications director for Unity Mississippi, on the steering committee of the Jackson, Mississippi, chapter of Parents, Friends, and Families of Lesbians and Gays (PFLAG), and in various other volunteer capacities. He has operated online communities since 1989. An internationally recognized expert on distance education (and coauthor of four books on the subject), Tom is currently finishing up his Ph.D. in the history of ideas at Edith Cowan University in Perth, Australia, through an off-campus study program.

Dedication

for Stacey Aldridge

Acknowledgments

I owe the existence of this book to my editor Rick Kughen, who gave me ideas when I ran out of ideas, imposed order on what was initially a pretty chaotic and unstructured book idea, and kept me moving when I got stuck. The words are mine, but the book is his. Cheers, Rick!

I am also grateful to my technical editor, Melody Drnach, whose expertise in the field of activism forced me to answer a crucially important question: What does this book *do*? Throughout this process, Melody kept my feet firmly planted on the ground and forced me to stay engaged and relevant vis-á-vis the real-life needs of activists.

I owe the existence of Tom Head to my parents, Carol Carwile Head and Cappy Page, and to my father, John Head. I owe the existence of Tom Head *as an activist* to my activism mentors, Shannan Reaze and Michelle Colón. I owe the existence of Tom Head as an author to my writing mentors, John and Mariah Bear.

And I owe so much of my confidence, my dignity, and my sanity to Stacey Aldridge, to whom this book is dedicated. She is, I can say without exaggeration, the best friend I have ever had. She has supported me for being who I am and challenged me to be a better person, all at the same time. She is also an exceptional activist, a brilliant writer, and a force for good in the world. Stacey, I love you.

There are many other people I can, and should, thank. But I can't name them all, and I dare not name only some of them. What I can say is that if you think I owe you my thanks, I almost certainly do; and if you think I owe you an apology for not mentioning you here, I almost certainly owe you that, too.

We Want to Hear from You!

As the reader of this book, *you* are our most important critic and commentator. We value your opinion and want to know what we're doing right, what we could do better, what areas you'd like to see us publish in, and any other words of wisdom you're willing to pass our way.

As an associate publisher for Que Publishing, I welcome your comments. You can email or write me directly to let me know what you did or didn't like about this book—as well as what we can do to make our books better.

Please note that I cannot help you with technical problems related to the topic of this book. We do have a User Services group, however, where I will forward specific technical questions related to the book.

When you write, please be sure to include this book's title and author as well as your name, email address, and phone number. I will carefully review your comments and share them with the author and editors who worked on the book.

Email: feedback@quepublishing.com

Mail: Greg Wiegand
            Associate Publisher
            Que Publishing
            800 East 96th Street
            Indianapolis, IN 46240 USA

Reader Services

Visit our website and register this book at informit.com/register for convenient access to any updates, downloads, or errata that might be available for this book.

"There is nothing new under the sun, but there are lots of old things we don't know."
—Ambrose Bierce

December 25th, 1990, was one of the most important dates in the history of American civil rights because that was the day that George Holliday got his first camcorder for Christmas.

George, a Los Angeles-area plumber who lived close enough to California's Interstate 210 to see the cars roll by, was out on his balcony a few months later, on March 3rd, when he saw something disturbing: four LAPD officers beating a black man. Holliday, who had spent time in Argentina and knew something about oppressive police tactics, did something the officers could not have anticipated: He whipped out his Sony HandyCam, took video, and distributed it to the media.

That's how we know Rodney King was beaten by the LAPD in 1991. That's why grassroots activists mobilized in protest against the beating. That's why the four officers were brought up on charges. That's why the L.A. riots ensued when the officers were acquitted. That's why federal charges were later filed against the officers. And that's why the Christopher Commission (which examined racism and civil rights abuses in the LAPD) came about later. The Commission's data and the controversy preceding it led to substantial, albeit inadequate, police reforms—not only within the LAPD, but also throughout the country. All this happened because George Holliday got a HandyCam for Christmas.

Now when police abuse citizens' civil rights, they have to be more careful about who's watching. When a group of undersupervised LAPD officers violently interrupted an immigration rally at MacArthur Park in May 2007, for example, they didn't just attack the protesters—they also attacked journalists and attempted to destroy TV cameras. Cell phone cameras, the Sony HandyCams of our age, captured it all on film. And when an Oakland police officer shot 22-year-old Oscar Grant in the back on New Year's Day 2009, despite the fact that Grant was unarmed, cooperative, and lying face down on the pavement, officers attempted to confiscate all nearby cell phone cameras as "evidence." A video taken by a young woman named Katrina Vargas, who eluded the search, quickly went public and prevented police from sweeping the incident under the rug.

Today, human rights activists focusing on police abuse at every level, and in every country, rely on the Internet and video technology to hold police accountable. WITNESS, founded by singer-songwriter Peter Gabriel in 1992 as a program of the Lawyers Committee for Human Rights, helps grassroots activists record and distribute video documenting human rights abuses perpetrated by oppressive governments. And a national network of "Copwatch" groups, in which citizens videotape police misconduct for purposes of grassroots activism and media distribution, help use technology to hold police accountable.

These changes in media technology are effective only when people are watching. Having a portable camera means that you can produce important documentation of civil rights abuses; it doesn't mean that you can distribute the evidence in a venue where people will actually see it. YouTube, for example, is full of videos of police beatings that never get media exposure nor substantial activist attention.

In November 2008, the largest gay rights rally in Mississippi history was held at the state capitol. It was organized by online activists, most of them out of state—a stunning success of online activism. But local media mostly ignored it, and the few local media outlets that did cover it largely underreported attendance. Attendees responded by uploading evidence of the rallies—photographs, videos, and firsthand accounts—to Facebook, MySpace, Flickr, YouTube, and other sites. The event wasn't just organized online; it was documented online. Traditional activism, and traditional media coverage, wasn't part of the picture.

Online activism is helpful even when you can recruit local media to help, but it's absolutely essential when you can't. Online activism bridges the gap between those who control media and those who do not. It allows us to organize events and membership, raise funds, and document actions. It gives us the ability to recruit activists—students, stay-at-home moms, night-shift workers, the severely disabled, and so forth—who have historically been underrepresented in traditional activism circles. It gives us the power to shape our world in innovative ways. It gives us the power to be the George Hollidays of our time.

About This Book

There was a time when a book like this would begin with statistics. I could cite Nielsen data from June 2008 indicating that 72.5% of Americans, or 220 million people, use the Internet. I could mention a 2009 Harvard study showing that online advertising is a $300 billion industry, accounting for more than two% of the U.S. Gross Domestic Product (GDP). I could refer to a July 2008 study from the Center for Philanthropy at Indiana University, suggesting that 12.6% of donations to nonprofit organizations take place over the Internet rather than through other means, or that 8% of organizations surveyed receive the majority of their donations online.

And I suppose I just did all of these things, but I didn't *have* to—because you already know the Internet is worth paying attention to. It's part of the American cultural mainstream now, its relevance established, its importance unchallenged. But it hasn't been that way for very long, and activist organizations have been relatively slow to get on the bandwagon.

I remember a presentation I gave in June 1997 on the importance of websites to nonprofit organizations. I argued that they represented permanent electronic real estate, that the Internet was growing, and that any organization that didn't need a website yet probably *would* need one over the coming years. All these predictions eventually came to pass, but my urgent and optimistic tone sounded ridiculous at the time, and I knew it. Convincing nonprofit leaders that a technology is worth pursuing can take years. The same Indiana University study showing that online donations make up 12.6% of overall donations, for example, also found that only 44% of nonprofits actually accept donations over the Internet. What percentage of donations would be given online if the other 56% of nonprofits followed suit?

People talk about "e-activism" and "online activism" as if they were new forms of activism, but they're really just new media for traditional forms of activism. True, they're revolutionary. But so was the telephone, and we don't still talk about "telephone activism"; it's understood that using a telephone as part of our activism efforts is normal. Online activism, or e-activism, will one day be perceived as normal, too.

Cover to Cover

This book is made up of ten chapters and five appendixes.

Chapter 1, "Online Activism 101," is your introduction to the world of online activism. I'll explain how to persuade traditional activists to use (or let you use) online media and how to use online media to support a cause on your own if they won't. I'll introduce your eight-part online activism toolkit (explored step-by-step in Chapters 2–9) and profile an organization that has used e-activism as a way to expand its reach, as well as an individual activist who has done a great deal of good online without the support of traditional activist groups.

Chapter 2, "How to Research Issues and Stay Informed," is all about using the Internet to *gather* information—part 1 of your eight-part online activism toolkit. I'll tell you how to use the Internet to research issues, monitor online newspapers and magazines to keep up with new developments on causes important to you, develop talking points, join relevant mailing lists and newsletters, avoid hoaxes and urban legends, find books and articles you need, keep up with legislation, legal codes, and court rulings, and use the Internet to connect with traditional resources such as reference librarians and interlibrary loan departments.

Chapter 3, "How to Build, Promote, and Maintain a Website," tells you how you can build and maintain a website—part 2 of your eight-part online activism toolkit. I'll explain how websites have traditionally been used to move activism forward and explain how you can tailor your website's content to meet the specific needs of local, non-local, and media readers. I'll also describe ways you can ethically promote your website and make it visible to the larger community, and share five tips on creating an activism website that's well worth having.

Chapter 4, "How to Use Social Networking Sites as an Activism," focuses on social networking—part 3 of your eight-part online activism toolkit. I'll describe the history of social networking (which connects very closely with the history of progressive activism), explain the advantages of social networking for activists, compare Facebook, MySpace, and other social networking services, highlight common mistakes that activists make when they use social networking services, and profile a political campaign that made the most of new social networking technology.

Chapter 5, "A Short Guide to the Ethics and Etiquette of Online Activism," deals with ethics and netiquette—part 4 of your eight-part online activism toolkit. I'll describe the 7 "deadly sins" of online activism, explain the difference between spam and legitimate site promotion, and tell you about the 10 most common types of offensively clueless online activists—and how to avoid becoming one of them.

Chapter 6, "How to Raise Funds, Host Contests, and Build Membership Online," deals with raising funds online—part 5 of your eight-part online activism toolkit. I'll talk about tools and services that nonprofits can use to process online donations, how to build up membership by offering members-only resources online, and how successful nonprofits have solicited funds online in the past. I'll profile an activist organization that has done very, very well with online donations.

Chapter 7, "How to Use Multimedia Technology as an Activism Tool," deals with multimedia technology—part 6 of your eight-part online activism toolkit. I'll review YouTube, Flickr, and other multimedia websites that can be useful to your cause, explain how and why and when to embed visual and audio content into your online activism materials, how to find online content that is public domain or can be used for free by nonprofits, and explain why podcasting *might* be a good idea. I'll also describe 10 cases where online multimedia was *central* to an activism effort.

Chapter 8, "How to Keep Allies Informed (Without Annoying Them Too Much)," deals with blogging and other technologies you can use to keep activists informed—part 7 of your eight-part online activism toolkit. I'll describe different blogging platforms and technologies, explain how RSS feeds work, go over the steps involved in creating an email newsletter or mailing list, describe how activists have used cell phone text messaging to organize volunteers and keep them informed, discuss online chat technologies, and review a wonderful little site called Twitter. I'll also describe five cases where blogging or other communication technologies were very helpful to an activism effort.

Chapter 9, "How to Create Effective Action Alerts and Online Petitions," deals with action alerts, online petitions, and other ways to use the Internet as a form of direct action. This is part 8—the last part of your eight-part activism toolkit. I'll discuss how to set up good action alerts (and how often to send them), address the issue of whether online petitions are a waste of time (and explain how you can make the most of them), address the issue of online polls, and go over other ways that you can use the Internet to directly organize activists. I also describe a case where an online petition did some good and profile an organization that has used action alerts very effectively.

Chapter 10, "How to Keep It Real," summarizes your eight-part online activism toolkit and explains how you can implement these strategies in the service of your own cause. I'll also go over some future and not yet widely adopted technologies that could significantly change the way we do online activism, describe how 10 organizations have used online activism in their work, and try to answer the question my activism mentor, Shannan Reaze, asked me in 2007: *Is* online activism killing "real" face-to-face activism? How can we make sure the two coexist effectively?

The appendixes are more important to this book, perhaps, than appendixes generally are. Appendix A sums up 10 common online activism mistakes and explains how to avoid them. Appendix B directs you to resources that you can use to find activism jobs and volunteer opportunities online. Appendix C is an illustrated timeline of online activism, from 125 BCE (yes, really) to mere days before this book went to press. Appendix D is a glossary of 100 common terms that online activists should know. And finally, Appendix E lists online degree programs that may be of interest to activists and those who work in the nonprofit sector.

Online Activism 101

"New technological environments are commonly cast in the molds of the preceding technology out of the sheer unawareness of their designers."

—Marshall McLuhan

I was standing in front of an easel in the middle of the windowless sanctuary of the Unitarian-Universalist Church of Jackson in June 1997, leading a forum discussion on the importance of online organizing for churches, and I looked like I was trying to sell something—and doing a terrible job of it.

"So why do we need a website?" one of the parishioners asked. It was a good question. I had no good answer because in 1997 only 22.1% of the U.S. population used the Internet—and Mississippi, America's poorest state and among its most rural, wasn't exactly leading the pack on early adoption (see U.S. Census Bureau, *Computer Use in the United States: Population Characteristics*, October 1997.)

I put up a good fight, but my argument wasn't convincing. I couldn't have even said "so people can Google us" because Google wasn't founded until a year later.

Now I'd be able to make a better case; three-quarters of the U.S. population uses the Internet, and access is almost universal at public libraries. At some point between 1997 and today, online organizing transformed from a possibility into an essential—from the next big thing to an indispensable part of your activism toolkit. It stopped being the business only of the kinds of innovators we see in Figure 1.1 and democratized. Today, the Internet belongs—or at least should belong—to everybody.

> > > **NOTE**

Technically, only 74.1% of the U.S. population uses the Internet, according to the August 2009 Nielsen Online NetRatings. I feel comfortable rounding this to 75% because in the period between August 2008 and August 2009, the figure went up from 72.5% to 74.1%. And Nielsen's numbers, the most reliable numbers we have, also tend to be the most conservative—a November 2007 Harris Poll, for example, claimed that 79% of Americans are Internet users.

Figure 1.1
The Ethos Roundtable, a group of Boston activists and technology experts, meets to discuss possible activism-related application of virtual reality technology. Photo: © 2006 Pathfinder Linden. Licensed under Creative Commons Attribution License 2.0 Generic.

Show me a national organization without a website, and I will show you a national organization with a very, very low level of national visibility. Having an online presence isn't just about being available on the Internet—it's about making facts available to non-Internet recruits, supporters, and media. If I want to know how many members the National Rifle Association has, I can go to www.nra.org and find out. If I want to give money to the Humane Society, I can go to www.hsus.org and donate. Everything I need is right there.

And as this book explores, there's so much more to a potential online activism presence than a simple website now. Armed with this book, you'll be ready to branch out into social media (see Chapter 4, "Engage with Social Networking Sites"), fundraising (see Chapter 6, "How to Raise Funds Online"), multimedia (see Chapter 7, "How to Use Multimedia as an Activism Tool"), blogging and newsletters (see Chapter 8, "How to Keep Allies Informed (Without Annoying Them Too Much)"), and online action alert campaigns (see Chapter 9, "Action Alerts and Online Petitions")—among other things. Your online activism campaign can engage people in many different ways.

In the C.S. Lewis novel, *Till We Have Faces*, a retelling of the Roman myth of Cupid and Psyche, a character laments:"How can the gods meet us face to face till we have faces?" And every opportunity a social movement misses to connect with people is another face it doesn't have.

Getting Started on the Internet

This book assumes you're new to online activism but not necessarily new to the Internet. If you're just getting into this new technology—and there's no shame in that—then a more general guide, such as *Michael Miller's Absolute Beginner's Guide to Computer Basics* (5th edition, Que Publishing, 2009), will tell you how to get online.

A New Tool, Not a New Project

Using online tools for activism sounds fancy, and there are quite a few fancy words people can use to describe it. E-activism. Cyberactivism. The list goes on. Each of these lovely new buzzwords sends the message that online activism is a different kind of activism, something new and exciting and vaguely magical that might or might not have anything to do with the kinds of activism you're used to.

Don't believe it, and don't let anybody intimidate you into believing that you can't use these tools effectively to promote your cause.

Online activism isn't some new, controversial form of activism; it's activism with new tools. We don't talk much about telephone activism, or radio activism, or print activism because we're used to those media. In time, online activism will be integrated, equally seamlessly, into the work we do—and books like this will look outdated, even a little bit silly.

But right now, we're at a unique moment in history where universal Internet access (see Figure 1.2) hasn't quite arrived. The technology is still new, most Americans still have a great deal to learn about it, and there's a culture-wide learning curve that we're all dealing with.

I wrote this book to help close that learning curve and put the power of online technology in your hands—but they're still your hands, and these are still just tools for you to use (or not use) as you see fit.

Figure 1.2
The computer room at Hoover Public Library in Birmingham, Alabama. Photo: © 2007 Elizabeth Swift. Licensed under Creative Commons Attribution License 2.0 Generic.

Where Do I Begin?

In my experience, most people who are interested in using online activism tools are either trying to use online activism as a branch of a traditional activist movement or trying to start a completely new activism initiative using online tools. Both approaches work, but they work in different ways.

Branching Out

This book is full of examples of traditional organizations that have used online activism to achieve their goals. In fact, you'll be hard pressed to find a major traditional activist group that doesn't use online tools to some degree.

The ACLU panel discussion shown in Figure 1.3, for example, was promoted online. The ACLU maintains a website (www.aclu.org), a blog and RSS feed (more on those in Chapter 8), an online fundraising campaign (more on those in Chapter 6), multiple social media accounts (more on those in Chapter 4), action alerts and online newsletters (more on those in Chapter 9), multimedia (more on those in Chapter 7), and so on.

Figure 1.3

A Los Angeles panel discussion on zero-tolerance policies in public schools, moderated by Catherine Kim of the American Civil Liberties Union (ACLU). Photo: © 2009 National Economic and Social Rights Initiative (NESRI). Licensed under Creative Commons Attribution License 2.0 Generic.

The ACLU has been around since 1920; it isn't an "e-activism" organization. But like most major organizations, it has made use of the Internet to achieve objectives that would have been impossible 10 years ago.

If you're trying to persuade a traditional activist organization to make better use of online tools, the first step is to look around, ask around, and make sure that people aren't already trying to do what you'd like to help the organization do. (If they are, and they aren't doing a particularly good job of it, they could probably use your help!) Once you've done that, there's a three-step process you can follow:

- **If you're new to the organization, approach friendly leaders quietly before you make any public offers**—If you can get somebody who is already established in the organization to pitch you instead of making the pitch yourself, your odds of bringing established activists on board with your idea increase considerably. I was placed in charge of local online activism and selected as public and community outreach chair at the very first National Organization for Women (NOW) meeting I ever attended because I had already approached the local chapter president quietly and asked to be put to work.

- **Be realistic about your expectations**—If you're the only person who is going to do any online activism for an organization, and you're not getting paid for it, you probably don't want to commit to the full spectrum of options described in this book. One volunteer shouldn't be expected to set up a website and promote events online and update a

Facebook page and maintain an email list and send out action alerts and so forth. Start small and add on new responsibilities only when you're sure you can handle the ones you've already committed to and remain happy and sane. And don't be afraid to share or delegate responsibilities.

- **If they're not interested, let it go**—you can help an organization become what it wants to be, but it isn't up to you to decide what it wants to be. If online activism isn't part of the existing member base's vision, you should respect that and move on.

Planting Seeds

The great community organizer Saul Alinsky wrote in his masterpiece *Rules for Radicals* (1971) that a movement's tactics depend on its size:

> [I]f you have organized a vast, mass-based people's organization, you can parade it visibly before the enemy and openly show your power ... [I]f your organization is small in numbers, then do what Gideon did: conceal the members in the dark but raise a din and clamor that will make the listener believe that your organization numbers many more than it does ... [I]f your organization is too tiny even for noise, stink up the place.
> —Saul Alinsky, *Rules for Radicals* (1971; Vintage, 1989), p. 126.

Thanks to the Internet, you don't necessarily have to stink up the place to get your message out. One of the nice things about online activism tools is that, frankly, they're pretty cheap. One person with the right skills, drive, and objective can make a bigger impact online than a multi-million dollar organization with a staff of hundreds. It doesn't happen often, but it does happen.

The left-wing progressive movement of the Bush years was primarily led by MoveOn.org, an organization that—as you can guess from its name—started off as a website. At first, it was a petition asking Republicans in Congress to "move on" from their investigation and attempted impeachment of President Bill Clinton in 1998. As time went on and the organization grew, the general progressive message of "moving on"—moving on from war, moving on from poverty, moving on from outmoded traditions, or just plain moving on—took over, and this initially small online group soon organized local meetups, rallies (see Figure 1.4), protests, letter-writing campaigns, and other traditional activism events.

MoveOn.org shows how online media can be the most fundamental tool of an activist movement in the same way the telephone or print mailings might be. The Internet isn't just a branch of MoveOn.org—it's the trunk.

Figure 1.4
A New Orleans rally in favor of universal healthcare, organized in part by MoveOn.org. Photo: © 2009 Bernard Pollack. Licensed under Creative Commons Attribution License 2.0 Generic.

No matter how small your movement is—even if it's just you—a well-timed, well-thought-out idea can travel online. Here are a few guidelines that I follow whenever I do online activism:

- **Stay focused**—If you want to do online activism on environmental issues, for example, don't randomly mix it up with online activism dealing with completely unrelated issues; that'll dilute your message.

- **Stay grounded in your community**—Attend relevant local face-to-face meetings, if you can, and work at building and maintaining the social connections that keep you in touch with other activists and make you more effective. Don't forget to promote traditional activism events, groups, and membership. The more you can align yourself with traditional power structures and traditional activism techniques, the more you can put these structures and techniques to the service of your cause.

- **Think global, act local**—Even if you're doing online activism, it's often best to focus on local issues. "It's a small world," stand-up comic Stephen Wright once remarked, "but I wouldn't want to have to paint it."

And take all of the above with a grain of salt because online activism is all about breaking new ground and being creative. MoveOn.org didn't follow any of these principles, and it changed the world. Maybe you will, too.

How to Research Issues and Stay Informed

"I'm sick and tired of hearing things from uptight, short-sighted, narrow-minded hypocrites.
All I want is the truth now.
Just gimme some truth."
—John Lennon

Let's face it: Online activism is mainly about spreading information. The Internet itself can't put feet on the ground, bills in front of the legislature, or voters in front of machines. It's just a tool that we use to spread information that helps people to do these things—so accuracy of information is key, as well as timeliness of information. The old adage that knowledge is power is even more literally relevant to an information-based medium than it is to the rest of the world because information is our currency, our product, and our greatest tool.

Technology writers tend to distinguish between Web 1.0 technology, where users act like audience members and essentially receive information, and Web 2.0 technology, where users can participate in information exchange. (Major conferences and think-tank events, such as the Web 2.0 Summit shown in Figure 2.1, have highlighted this distinction.) A Web 1.0 approach to video sharing, for example, is Hulu.com, where media companies distribute videos to users. But a Web 2.0 approach to video sharing is YouTube, where individual users can share videos with each other on more-or-less equal footing with any media companies that choose to participate.

Figure 2.1
Al Gore (center) joins other scholars specializing in online communities at the annual Web 2.0 Summit in 2008. Photo: © 2008 Mathieu Ramage. Licensed under Creative Commons Attribution License 2.0 Generic.

Most of this book focuses on the participatory Web 2.0 approach—but there's still plenty of content out there on the Internet that's just meant to be read, received, and digested. Most of it is self-explanatory, but this chapter will walk you through the basics of how you can use the Internet to conduct basic research and harvest information.

Lies My Inbox Told Me

False information travels just as fast as accurate information, and sometimes it travels faster. An inaccurate chain letter can undo months of advocacy, and getting your facts wrong in an action alert is one of the most reliable ways to turn off other activists.

If you're looking for the truth, you're probably not going to find it in chain letters—but they're not all phony. So how can you separate the wheat from the chaff? By doing a little research.

Snopes.com is the Web's leading resource on chain letters and urban legends—the true, the false, and the simply unverifiable. Although no site is 100% reliable, Snopes comes close.

And if Snopes doesn't have anything to say about your latest chain letter, About.com: Urban Legends (http://urbanlegends.about.com) probably will.

The important thing to bear in mind is not to forward along unsourced rumors, chain letters, and other unverified information. That can quickly destroy your credibility as an activist.

General Resources

Most users find what they're looking for by using a search engine (most commonly Google, as shown in Figure 2.2, at www.google.com), and this is usually the best way to begin researching a topic online. If you want information on death penalty statistics in Mississippi, for example, typing the phrase "death penalty statistics mississippi" into the Google search field turns up a website from the Mississippi Department of Corrections that includes death penalty statistics. Google also includes many other Internet services under its corporate umbrella, most of them search-related (see Table 2.1). Other popular search engines include Microsoft Bing (www.bing.com) and Yahoo! Search (search.yahoo.com).

Figure 2.2
Vendors prepare the Google booth at E-Commerce Expo 2008 in London, England. Google's color scheme and marketing strategy (which includes large doses of humor) contribute to its approachability, which may be as essential to its success as the actual effectiveness of its search engine. Photo: © 2008 Sam Greenhalgh. Licensed under Creative Commons Attribution License 2.0 Generic.

Google's basic search engine (www.google.com) isn't the only way to access information through the site—and it isn't always the most efficient or powerful, either. Google offers many specialized tools outside of its general search engine, and most of the ones shown in Table 2.1 can at least occasionally prove useful in an activism context.

Table 2.1   THE GOOGLE WITH A THOUSAND FACES

Service	URL	Function
Google Alert	alert.google.com	Sends you realtime links to news stories and other new online content that mentions your keyword phrase. For example: If you want an email alert every time somebody mentions both "abortion" and "mississippi" in a new article or web page, along with a link to the relevant piece of content, Google Alert will facilitate that.
Google Blog Search	blogsearch.google.com	Specifically searches blogs. Blogs are also archived as part of the main Google search engine.
Google Books	books.google.com	Accesses millions of digitized books, all text-searchable through Google.
Google Calendar	www.google.com/calendar	Allows users to create and search calendars.
Google Directory	www.google.com/dirhp	Google interacts with the Open Directory Project (www.dmoz.org), which archives many web pages organized by topic.
Google Docs	docs.google.com	Collaborative word processing and document editing through Google.
Google Earth	earth.google.com	Visual search of the planet Earth, using satellite data and on-the-ground photography.
Google Groups	groups.google.com	Search the archives of, create, and participate in online discussion forums—including Usenet newsgroups.
Google Health	health.google.com	Allows users to store their medical records in a central, web-accessible location.
iGoogle	www.google.com/ig	Allows users to create a customized homepage that links to other web content.
Google Images	images.google.com	Searches web images rather than text.
Google Maps	maps.google.com	Similar to Mapquest (www.mapquest.com), Google Maps will provide directions from one location to another—or allow users to browse street maps all over the world.
Google News	news.google.com	News-specific search engine.
Google Product Search	www.google.com/products	An online catalog search engine.
Google Reader	www.google.com/reader	The best web-based RSS feed browser.
Google Scholar	scholar.google.com	Searches journal articles and academic volumes.
Google Talk	www.google.com/talk	Online chat client.
Google Translate	translate.google.com	Similar to Babelfish (babelfish.yahoo.com), Google Translate will let users browse English translations of foreign-language web sites.
Google Videos	video.google.com	Searches web videos rather than text. Integrated with YouTube (www.youtube.com), which has since been purchased by Google.
Google Wave	www.googlewave.com	Online realtime document collaboration and chat client.

But there are times when you don't know exactly what you're looking for, in which case general Internet directories—essentially libraries of links, organized by general topic—can be much more helpful. These days, the best are probably the Yahoo! Directory (http://dir.yahoo.com), the Open Directory Project (www.dmoz.org), and the Google Directory (http://directory.google.com). These can be especially useful if you're looking for a national or international organization dedicated to a specific issue. (Yahoo! was once *just* an Internet directory, and the only general Internet directory that most people used, but it has since branched out; see Table 2.2)

Yahoo! (www.yahoo.com) is still one of the largest and most popular Internet corporations. While it is no longer gatekeeper to the Internet—that role has been largely taken over by Google—it remains an important tool.

Table 2.2   USEFUL YAHOO SERVICES

Service	URL	Function
Yahoo!	www.yahoo.com	User-defined portal to online information.
Yahoo! Alerts	alerts.yahoo.com	Similar to Google Alerts (alerts.google.com), Yahoo! Alerts updates you on any new content that matches your user-defined keyword phrases.
Yahoo! Answers	answers.yahoo.com	User-submitted questions and answers. Often helpful, sometimes terribly unhelpful.
Yahoo! Creative Commons Search	search.yahoo.com/cc	Searches copylefted, royalty-free content that you can use in your activist organization. For more on Creative Commons and other copylefted/royalty-free content, see Chapter 7.
Yahoo! Language Tools	babelfish.yahoo.com	Babelfish allows users to translate text and web pages from one language into another.
Yahoo! Maps	maps.yahoo.com	Similar to Mapquest (www.mapquest.com) and Google Maps (maps.google.com), Yahoo! Maps allows users to read street maps and generate directions from one location to another.
Yahoo! Search	search.yahoo.com	Yahoo!'s competitor to Google.

Although it's not, strictly speaking, a directory—and can be edited by anyone, introducing the possibility of serious errors—Wikipedia (www.wikipedia.org) is a great place to research topics. Most Wikipedia entries also have an External Links heading at the bottom, where you can find more online resources.

Print Publications

Although electronic text is slowly replacing desiccated tree carcasses as the print medium of choice, the printing press has had a 1,100-year head start. Most of the material that has been written and published throughout human history isn't available electronically—and what is available isn't always easy to find in search engines or web directories. (Indeed, as shown in Figure 2.3, it is not necessarily easy to find at all.)

Figure 2.3
In this 1910 photograph, students at a New York City public library research and study their subjects. For most children growing up in the United States today, research doesn't look like this at all—it involves more computer searches and less reliance on browsing print media, more research that can be done at home and less that needs to be done onsite at a library. Photo: Public domain, courtesy of the Library of Congress.

If you're looking for information that might be in a print book, you can search the full text of millions of books for free by using Google Book Search (http://books.google.com), Europeana (www.europeana.eu), and Amazon.com's full text search feature (www.amazon.com). And if you'd just like to read up on a subject and are looking for a publicly available book about it, the Digital Book Index (www.digitalbookindex.org) links to about 150,000 free online texts. Most, being in the public domain, are fairly old—but could still be of interest.

For more recent texts, particularly academic texts, the $19.95/month service Questia (www.questia.com) archives more than 70,000 books and two million articles, many of them recent. You can also find academic articles by using Google Scholar (http://scholar.google.com), Google's academic search engine. For nonacademic articles, your best bet is probably BNET's FindArticles.com (www.findarticles.com) or the MagPortal article search engine (www.magportal.com).

Laws and Legislation

If your activism includes lobbying, action alerts, or other policy work, you'll need to keep an eye on active legislation.

For federal law, you can find the Constitution and U.S. Code hosted in a wonderfully accessible, searchable format at Cornell University's School of Law (www4.law.cornell.edu/uscode/). You can also find a database of U.S. Supreme Court rulings from 1893 to the present, searchable and organized by topic, at FindLaw (www.findlaw.com/casecode/supreme.html). For the most recent opinions and the Court docket you can go to the Supreme Court's own official website (www.supremecourtus.gov/). And for the full text of federal legislation, updated frequently, check out the Library of Congress THOMAS legislation directory (http://thomas.loc.gov/).

At the state level, things are only slightly trickier. Cornell University maintains a directory of state law databases (www.law.cornell.edu/states/listing.html), but there is no comparable directory of state supreme courts; your best bet is to go to Google and type the state name and the phrase "supreme court" (or, if that doesn't immediately provide you with a useful match, try "superior court" instead). For pending state legislation, the National Conference of State Legislators maintains a national directory of resources (www.ncsl.org/public/leglinks.cfm). Although plenty of counties and municipalities have their laws available online, the best way to find them is—once again—to Google the cities and counties individually.

> > > **NOTE**

> Want to keep up with state ballot initiatives? The Ballot Initiative Strategy Center (www.ballot.org) is the best place to start.

Keeping Up with News Sites and Blogs

Good activism is mindful of the past, but it doesn't stay there. The objective of activism is to act—to get things done (or undone) in the real world.

And that means good information. Fortunately, most major newspapers have articles online for free now. News aggregator sites, most notably Google News (http://news.google.com) and Yahoo! News (http://news.yahoo.com), archive recent stories from newsletters all over the planet and make them searchable based on topics and searchable phrases. Both also allow users to create custom news home pages tailored to specific interests or keywords. Some web aggregators, most notably Digg (www.digg.com) and Delicious (www.delicio.us), are "social bookmarking" sites that rank news stories based on the number of votes given to them by users.

The blogosphere spreads out over wider, less visible terrain, but various tools can help you maneuver your way around it. One of the more useful is Technorati (www.technorati.com), the most widely used blog database, although Google Blog Search (http://blogsearch.google.com/) can also be helpful.

Alternative and independent media is a must for activists because corporate media does not always reliably cover the stories you need to hear about. (This has always been the case, as shown in Figure 2.4) The most productive sources of investigative journalism for activists are the 123 papers that make up the Association of Alternative Newsweeklies (www.aan.org), and if you live in the United States, there's probably one near you. The Independent Media Center (www.indymedia.org) is also a good source of international noncorporate news.

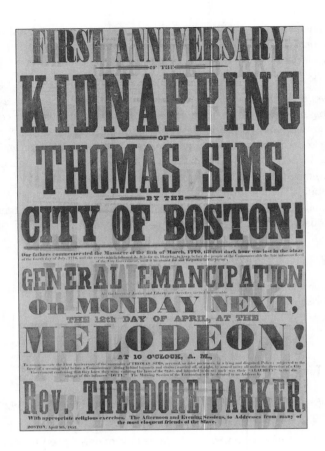

Figure 2.4
*Abolitionist newspapers of the 1850s, such as the one shown here, covered the antislavery move-
ment, abuse of slaves, and other topics that mainstream newspapers of the period often neglected.
Photo: Public domain, courtesy of the Library of Congress.*

The Wikimedia Foundation has also gotten into the act. In addition to Wikipedia itself
(www.wikipedia.org), which is a great source of reference material and is generally updated
often enough to be relevant to current news, the Foundation also hosts Wikinews
(www.wikinews.org), a news site, and WikiLeaks (www.wikileaks.com), which features censored
and classified government documents from every country.

Whether you're reading news sites or blogs, keeping up with a large number of sites can be a
challenge. Fortunately, if you're monitoring sites that offer an RSS feed (and the vast majority
of blogs and news sites do), it's possible to keep track of all new articles and blog posts on a
single page without having to visit every site you're interested in keeping track of (see
www.whatisrss.com for details).

Other Ways to Keep Track of Breaking News

You can stay on top of breaking news in other ways, too. To name a few

- **Watch what other activists are posting on social networks**—For more on social networking, see Chapter 4.
- Subscribe **to relevant Twitter feeds**—For more on Twitter, see Chapter 8.
- Subscribe to action alert distribution listservs—For more about action alerts, see Chapter 9.

Your E-Activism Toolkit: Getting Informed

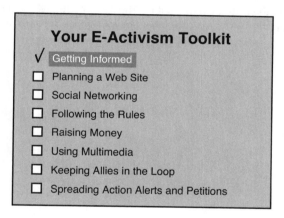

Activism is primarily about *doing* things. Researching and staying informed about topics is important, but it isn't exactly activism in and of itself. But a central element of good activism is that it speaks truth to power, and if you don't know what the truth is, that's hard to do. This is why getting informed is the first part of your e-activism toolkit.

However, nobody changes the world very much just by reading media. You can change the world by *producing* media, but you can't really change the world by reading it. So the key is to develop an efficient strategy for keeping up with the news and, as much as is practical, stick to it.

Every activist group, formal or informal, has people within it who are more aware than most of what is going on in terms of relevant news and blog content. If you don't know who those people are—if you don't feel like there are people in your movement who keep you in the loop—then you need to be one of those people yourself.

How you do this will depend on what kind of activism you do. If you're a local activist, you will probably rely primarily on local newspapers. If there's an alternative weekly nearby (see www.aan.org), that will probably be the activism media center of your community. Be sure to also keep an eye on your local daily newspaper; they're still the most prolific news sources. Unless you live in a very large community such as New York City or the Bay Area, blogs are *not* especially likely to be your main source of local activism news—but be sure to check and see if any relevant ones exist.

If you're doing activism on national or international causes, you will probably rely more on blogs and organizational newsletters and less on general media sites. National news sites are not, as a rule, especially interesting or useful for activists who specialize in a particular topic or cluster of topics. Find five blogs that represent your general area of focus and are updated enough to be useful for you, subscribe to their RSS feeds, and read them regularly. Change.org (www.change.org) is also a good site to bookmark, as it maintains a fairly extensive collection of subject-specific pages related to popular activist causes.

And don't overlook magazines. I won't make any specific suggestions because they'll vary depending on what your topic is, but if you know people in your area of activism (and this is essential—if you don't know any, meet some), they can make you aware of the national media outlets that publish the most useful content in your field.

But don't get too bogged down in knowing it all. The important thing, from an activism point of view, is more to *tell* the truth than to dig it up. The next chapter tells you how to begin this process by setting up the most basic component of your online activism presence: a website.

How to Plan, Promote, and Maintain a Website

"Content is king."—Internet marketing aphorism

No matter what else you do online, odds are very good that it will revolve around a website designed to keep supporters up to date—a website that anchors the various kinds of content you produce elsewhere online and that provides a semipermanent location for reference information about your organization or cause. Having a website, in and of itself, doesn't do much good; what makes a website useful is the content it organizes and presents.

What This Book Will Not Tell You

If you're looking for information on how to code HTML and CSS, this is the wrong book for that. Try Julie Meloni and Michael Morrison's *Sams Teach Yourself HTML and CSS in 24 Hours* (8th edition, 2010) instead.

And this is key—content must come first. People talk a lot about web design, and it can be useful to know how to make a gorgeous website, but ultimately the purpose of a website is to present and provide a structural framework for content. So before you design a website, the important thing is to decide what to put on it—and not necessarily how the site will be presented.

There are many possible answers to the question, "What belongs on an organizational website?" But the more crucial question is: What are your likely readers going to want to see on your organization's website? What kind of information will they need?

In other words, what is your website for?

Finding Your Audience

Most organizational websites are read primarily by three groups of people: local supporters, nonlocal supporters, and media. Each has different, but overlapping, needs.

Organizing Local Supporters

If you're involved in a local organization or the local branch of a national organization or if you're advocating a cause and need more local people to help out, a website can help get them organized.

But as I discuss in Chapter 10, "It's Your World, So Change It," the purpose of online content for local supporters is most often to empower them to get off the Internet and out into the local activist community.

Local supporters need the following:

- **Contact information that emphasizes traditional forms of communication**—Local supporters are more likely to visit your organization's office or call your organization on the telephone than nonlocal supporters are.

- **Participation-oriented information that emphasizes events**—If you have any events to publicize, local supporters are likely to make up most of your attendees—and this will be their primary vehicle for social and emotional connection with your organization. Your information on events should be tailored primarily for local supporters, and your website, to the extent that it focuses on local supporters, should be primarily geared toward getting them to attend your events.

- **Action alerts and talking points with local relevance**—If local supporters are your primary intended audience, it makes sense to focus primarily on local issues and the impact of national issues on your local community. If I'm writing an activism website promoting a national universal health care plan in Mississippi, for example, local supporters are going to be interested in knowing how many Mississippians are uninsured in addition to, or instead of, the national statistics you tend to see cited in national media outlets. (For more on action alerts, see Chapter 8, "How to Keep Allies and Supporters in the Loop.")

- **Coalitioning with other local groups**—Local activism is the most socially dependent kind of online activism; you will have to rely on word-of-mouth and allied organizations to recruit supporters, and the more activists you send to other local organizations, the more likely those other local organizations are to send activists to you.

Case Study: Coalition on Homelessness, San Francisco (www.cohsf.org)

According to the San Francisco Homeless Services Coalition, approximately 35,000 homeless people live in the Bay Area at any given time. Both religious and secular organizations provide some direct services to the homeless, but the San Francisco Homeless Services Coalition takes a different approach by organizing and advocating on homelessness-related civil rights issues on a policy level.

While the COHSF website is exceptionally solid and illustrates all the preceding principles, it is also very simple and basic in its layout. It's very clear that it exists primarily to direct local activists to the on-the-ground work of the organization, and anyone who uses the site will immediately know how to get involved in its work.

Using the Main Page to Control Your Local Message

Most commercial websites are busy, full of linked content, advertisements, and logos. But organizational websites, especially local ones, are often more spartan—which means that what they do feature is given greater significance.

The main page (shown in Figure 3.1) zeroes in on three things: a paragraph description of the organization, information on an upcoming event, and information on a study that includes local data. The message it sends is of an organization that is action-focused and participatory, and readers are given a subtle message: Here's what we do; here's where you can go to do something productive if you care about it; here's information you can use to further educate yourself about the cause.

Figure 3.1
The main website of the Coalition on Homelesseness, San Francisco.

The message it sends, in other words, is that the organization is about things you're (hopefully) about to do and things you need to know.

Now imagine if, instead of information on an event and a research report, the page provided information on an event that had already happened, accompanied by a photograph and bio of the executive director. What message would that send? It would send the message that the organization is primarily about things that other people have already done and other people who are already in the organization.

One approach provides an avenue for the visitor and potential supporter. The other provides no real avenues; it's fluff.

This is not to say that information on staff and past events have no place on a local organizational web page—but they should not be the central focus of the website, and they should not be the only featured content on the main page. Use your home page, your front door, to immediately engage readers and give them some ideas on what they can do next.

Watch Your Language

You'll notice a link in the lower-left corner of the page shown in Figure 3.1: "Oprime aqui para ver este sitio en español." Click it, and you get the Spanish version of the page—essential if you're trying to organize homeless folks in the Bay Area, where 21% of the population is Latino and Latinos represent a disproportionately high percentage of the poor.

If a significant percentage of your likely readers probably speak another language better than they speak English, and if you have someone who speaks the relevant language(s) well enough to prepare a translation, it makes a lot of sense to provide a translation of your page.

The left column provides further information on the organization. About the Coalition on Homelessness, for example, provides the sort of basic necessary, but unengaging, information about the organization (history, organizational philosophy, structure) that most local organizations would put on their front page, but usually shouldn't. Workgroups goes into specific areas where the COHSF does its work. The three links below the Workgroups section give local supporters even more ways to get involved: by attending a meeting (Meeting Schedule), by donating (Support Our Work), or by getting in touch with the organization (Contact Us).

Let's focus on that Contact Us link because the way this organization handles its contact information is remarkable.

Your Organization's Physical Presence

Remember how I mentioned earlier in this chapter that local organizations are usually well served to emphasize traditional ways of contacting the group—showing up or telephoning—rather than relying exclusively on online contact information? Let's look at how the COHSF does that and in the process capitalizes on the fact that most of its base of support is local.

Note that the Contact Us page (shown in Figure 3.2) provides not only the physical address of the building, but also directions that would be useful for Bay Area residents ("between Hyde and Larkin"). Note that the page instructs visitors to ring the doorbell to get buzzed in—something that only someone who shows up at the building would need to know. Note that the page mentions which days the organization is not open, so people don't waste a trip trying to come by on one of those days.

Figure 3.2

Contact Us page for the Coalition on Homelessness, San Francisco

Note also the employee-specific contact information—a sure sign that the organization is transparent, accountable to its constituents, and wants people to contact it. Incidentally, this is the only place on the website where the executive director's name is even mentioned—she is not referred to at all on the About page. This is a very humble approach, one that your organization may not need to emulate to this extent, but it reminds visitors that the executive director is there to work and expects your primary interaction with her to be participatory. She does not rule over the organization from on high, issuing pronouncements to supporters but otherwise remaining more or less invisible. She is actually in the field. This makes the organization seem friendly, open, and focused on getting things done.

There is, of course, email contact information—and both local and nonlocal supporters might use it. But the fact that the website doesn't shy away from traditional modes of contact is very empowering and no doubt helps the organization recruit supporters.

Now let's look at that Meeting Schedule link, the third from the bottom on the left.

Local Meetings

Committed local supporters tend to be face-to-face supporters, and the art auction promoted on the main page will help draw them in. But what if they can't make it to the art auction, aren't interested in the art auction, or want to do something on a more regular basis after it's over?

Most local organizations don't have enough staff to organize five substantive topic-specific meetings every week—34 hours of regular meetings every month, in the case of COHSF (see Figure 3.3)—but if your organization has a regular meeting and you want as many people as possible to know about it, listing it on the website is a great idea. In fact, unless you've got a user-friendly event (like an art auction!) coming up soon, it might not be a bad idea to feature your next meeting on the main page.

Figure 3.3
Meeting Schedule page for the Coalition on Homelessness, San Francisco.
http://www.cohsf.org/en/meetingSchedule.php (accessed August 23, 2009)

Alongside the upcoming event promotion on the main page is a link to a new report on an issue important to the organization's constituents: the San Francisco shelter reservation system.

Fact Sheets, Reports, and Talking Points

The Coalition's main page highlights a new report titled "The Runaround: An Examination of San Francisco's Byzantine Shelter Reservation System," which interviews 212 shelter clients who have been affected, most often negatively, by attempts to streamline the city's homeless shelter system. The report is timely, providing context for a recent overhaul of the system that could improve or diminish the experiences of homeless clients.

But it's just one issue. For other data, you can click Reports and Fact Sheets on Homeless—the first link on the main page's left column—and get the Reports page (shown in Figure 3.4). This series of research-intensive reports is much more academic and detailed than anything that would fall within the purview of most local organizations, but it provides a useful model for structuring locally relevant documents: highlight a single issue that the organization is focusing on right now, while providing easily accessible links to resources on other issues. Don't try to feature every document or fact sheet the organization has ever produced on the main page. Yes, it makes the organization look productive—but it can be a headache for users.

Figure 3.4
The Reports page featureed on the website of the Coalition on Homelessness, San Francisco.

This basic principle applies to all the content on websites tailored to local supporters: Keep it simple, keep it breezy, and don't make it any more intimidating than you have to.

Nonlocal Supporters

Your website's approach to nonlocal supporters is likely to differ from its approach to local supporters in that most of their interaction with your organization will probably be online. With local activism, online activism is usually the drawbridge to the castle; with nonlocal activism, online activism usually is the castle. Your organization's most dedicated supporters may be people you'll meet face-to-face at regional events, but they're not likely to be the primary audience for your website—and are certainly not likely to make up most of its audience.

For this reason, websites that rely heavily or mostly on nonlocal support have to be a little bit tighter. You can get away with a local organizational website that's basically a regularly updated online flyer if you're just using it as a way to draw them into traditional venues, but people from out of state are not going to be satisfied with that because the website is their traditional venue.

If you're running a local organization, or the local chapter of a national organization, local supporters should probably be your priority. But if you're trying to organize people to address a national problem, or organize a national group of people to address local problems, or write a general website for a national organization, then your website is going to be the organization's center of gravity.

Nonlocal supporters need the following:

- **Contact information that emphasizes online communication**—Nonlocal supporters might call, snail mail, or even visit your organization—so it makes sense to provide the contact information somewhere—but they probably won't. If they're looking at your website, they're already Internet literate; why not fill out a form or send an email? It's much more convenient.

- **Support-oriented information that emphasizes donations and opportunities for follow-up contact**—Local supporters can provide on-the-ground support, but nonlocal supporters generally can't. This means that the two best ways they can support your organization are very probably by sending your organization money and making themselves available to participate in future online campaigns by subscribing to an email mailing list or newsletter and/or joining a social networking group dedicated to your organization. (For more on raising funds online, see Chapter 6. For more on keeping other activists informed, see Chapter 8.)

- **Action alerts and talking points with national relevance**—National websites tend to do better if they focus on national issues or on local issues that are outrageous or interesting enough to generate national interest.

- **Unique, value-added content**—National organizational websites don't necessarily have to be fun to use (though it sure helps), but they do need to be pleasant to use. If other organizational websites address the same issue(s), you are effectively competing for attention—and will need to offer something that online users will want to look at.

Case Study: ColorOfChange.org (www.colorofchange.org)

When you think of national activism, you might think of MoveOn.org—the online activism group founded during the Clinton impeachment proceedings in 1998. But MoveOn.org has gotten so big and has become such a broad-based left-wing institution that using it as a model for nonlocal activism probably isn't practical.

A more focused, useful example might be ColorOfChange.org, cofounded in the aftermath of Hurricane Katrina by MoveOn.org's former online community organizer James Rucker (see Figure 3.5). ColorOfChange.org, the largest institution in the online third wave of the African-American civil rights movement, targets racial profiling, corporate support of racist rhetoric, and economic injustice. As the organizational mission statement puts it:

ColorOfChange.org is strengthening Black America's political voice. Using the Internet, we keep our members informed and give them ways to act on pressing issues facing Black people in America. We are united behind a simple, powerful pledge: We will do all we can to make sure all Americans are represented, served, and protected—regardless of race or class.

Like the Coalition on Homelessness, ColorOfChange.org's web design is simple in a way that contributes to its effectiveness.

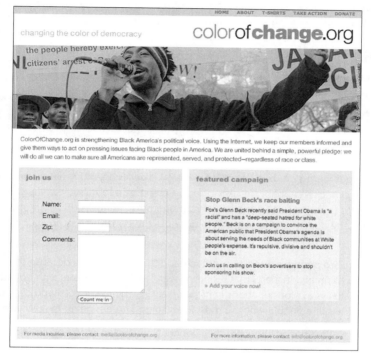

Figure 3.5
Main website of ColorOfChange, a civil rights e-activism organization.

It doesn't get much better than this, folks.

The content of the page tells you what the organization is and the main thing it wants you to do, gives you a form to join, and gives you discreet opportunities (in the top column of the page) to learn more about the organization, buy a T-shirt, check up on other action alerts, or donate. I'll go more into how to deal with web forms and action alerts in Chapter 9, but they're essential to websites that rely on nonlocal participation. You can't just ask for money. People need other ways to connect, too.

The only things I'd add to this page are prominent links to social networking group pages (I'll go more into social networking in the next chapter), but ColorOfChange.org doesn't really need them at this point because its email newsletter (which people can join by filling out the Join Us form on the left of the main page) already does a good job of networking its nonlocal supporters. (I'll talk about email newsletters more in Chapter 8.)

The front pages of most national organizations' websites are busier than this, containing more links and pictures and so forth, but this doesn't necessarily work to their advantage. What a commenter on Alison Doyle's About.com Job Searching site said about cover letters also applies to the main page on an organizational website: Putting all your links on the main page is like forgetting to tie your bathrobe. No matter how proud you are of your stuff, you need to control the rate of exposure.

ColorOfChange.org hits the perfect balance. In some situations it pays to have a busier website than this, but not in very many situations. If you're just starting out, this is about as complicated as you want your design to be—and if you can keep it this simple, focused, and approachable for the long haul without sacrificing your message, you should.

Now, about that Donate link on the upper right…

Soliciting Donations

Asking for money online is always a little tricky. But not asking for money and then having inadequate funds to run your organization is even trickier.

I talk more about raising funds in Chapter 6—PayPal is necessary; information for people who want to pay by check is probably necessary; and a credit card form, such as the one shown in Figure 3.6, helps (but requires a secure server, among other things). But if your organization accepts funds, the question of how much to promote the donation link on your main page is a valid one.

ColorOfChange.org prefers a discreet approach, and this makes sense because the organization is so focused on action alerts that it doesn't want to distract visitors with donation information. It can always ask for donations in its newsletters—which people who care about the organization, the same people who are most likely to donate, are going to read anyway.

But there's no real harm in putting a bigger Donate Now button or the equivalent on your main page. Just remember that the people most likely to donate are also those most likely to scan the page for a Donate link anyway, so my guess—there have been no real studies on this that I'm aware of—is that the point of diminishing returns for main-page donation links is pretty low. The more important goal is to project the image of an organization that's worth donating to, and ColorOfChange.org does that in spades by focusing on action alerts.

As I discuss more in Chapter 10, online activism isn't really about new activism. It's about breaking down frustrating barriers to old activism.

The first ingredient to effective activism is to describe a problem, and the second ingredient is to provide an avenue for people to participate in the solution. Those heartbreaking commercials with starving kids exist so that you'll get emotionally engaged enough to actually sponsor a kid's meals, get involved in the work of the ONE Foundation (www.one.org), or take other measures to feed those starving kids you see in the commercials.

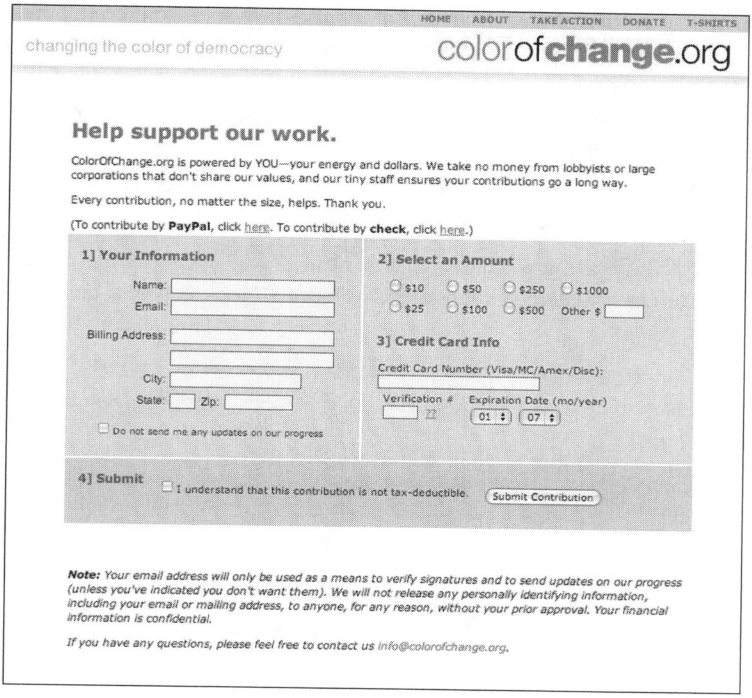
HOME ABOUT TAKE ACTION DONATE T-SHIRTS

changing the color of democracy colorofchange.org

Help support our work.

ColorOfChange.org is powered by YOU—your energy and dollars. We take no money from lobbyists or large corporations that don't share our values, and our tiny staff ensures your contributions go a long way.

Every contribution, no matter the size, helps. Thank you.

(To contribute by **PayPal**, click here. To contribute by **check**, click here.)

1] Your Information

Name:
Email:
Billing Address:
City:
State: Zip:
Do not send me any updates on our progress

2] Select an Amount

$10 $50 $250 $1000
$25 $100 $500 Other $

3] Credit Card Info

Credit Card Number (Visa/MC/Amex/Disc):
Verification # ?? Expiration Date (mo/year) 01 07

4] Submit I understand that this contribution is not tax-deductible. Submit Contribution

***Note:** Your email address will only be used as a means to verify signatures and to send updates on our progress (unless you've indicated you don't want them). We will not release any personally identifying information, including your email or mailing address, to anyone, for any reason, without your prior approval. Your financial information is confidential.*

If you have any questions, please feel free to contact us info@colorofchange.org.

Figure 3.6

Donation page for ColorOfChange.org.

Anger, horror, shock, fear, guilt, sadness—in their proper context, these are all positive emotions because they motivate change and save lives. Your goal as an activist is not to make people happy—not in the short run. It's to make people a little less happy, a little less satisfied, so that they're forced to get involved in solving the problem that upsets them in order to feel better. You want to be the site that people have to get out of bed and fill out the form for, or donate to, so they can sleep. Yes, you're manipulating people's emotions—because the human cost of not manipulating people's emotions is too high.

There's a lot of discussion in activism about the importance of "taking their blinders off." But have you ever wondered why horses wear blinders to begin with? It's so they can keep moving forward without getting spooked by what's going on in their periphery. Human blinders operate in much the same way. We wouldn't be able to keep going forward as happy, emotionally healthy, productive people if we were always fully conscious of the suffering and injustice that goes on around us. Taking people's blinders off isn't a very nice thing to do, and there isn't even any point to doing it unless we're prepared to show people a way they can change the suffering and injustice around them enough to satisfy their feelings of guilt, put their blinders back on, and move forward once again.

We have an obligation to identify problems. But we also have an obligation to provide avenues, to provide vehicles, to solve these problems. Doing this through nonlocal online activism is challenging because it deprives us of all the usual avenues for taking a stand and feeling like we've done something productive—protests, grassroots lobbying, and other opportunities to physically identify with a cause.

Action alerts, which I'll discuss more in Chapter 9, provides a less satisfying alternative to traditional protests—but it at least gives people something constructive to do with all those negative feelings, an open field for us spooked horses to run on.

ColorOfChange.org has mastered action alerts. In Figure 3.7 look, in particular, at the second entry down.

Figure 3.7
ColorOfChange.org's "Highlighted Campaigns" page.

By the time you've read a few sentences into the description shown in Figure 3.8 and looked at the photo, you're hooked. Click the link, and there's a little form you can fill out that will send a letter to the local district attorney asking for an investigation. Filling out a form changes this situation from one that merely frustrates you, that makes you shrug your shoulders, to one that you can personally take measures to change. That's activism because it allows you to act to change a given situation.

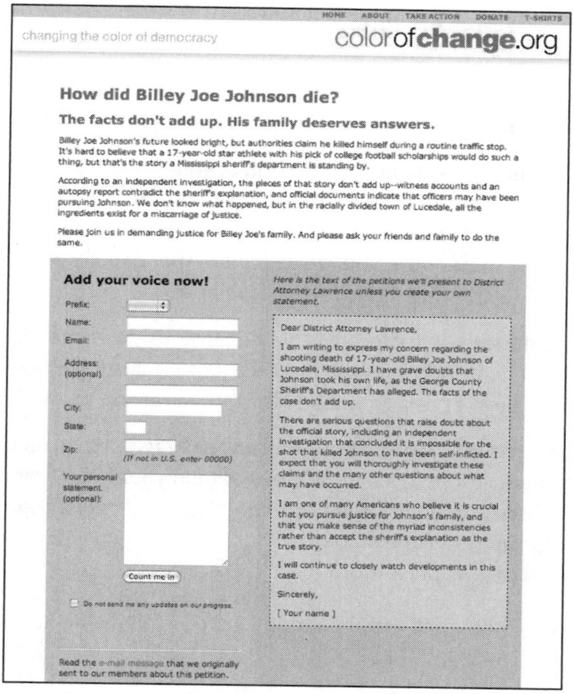

Figure 3.8
ColorOfChange's page on the suspicious death of Billey Joe Johnson.

Whether you use action alerts or not, always give people a pressure valve. Always give them something constructive they can do to become part of the solution. This is especially important with nonlocal activists, who will not be able to address their emotional needs or sustain their emotional investment by becoming part of a local activist community.

Making Your Website Media Friendly

In 2006, marketing scholars Bryan Reber and Jun Kyo Kim wrote an extensively researched piece for the *Journal of Public Relations Research* titled "How Activist Groups Use Websites in Media Relations: Evaluating Online Press Rooms." Their findings were not encouraging:

> About one-third of activist websites include elements that would especially encourage return visits. In addition to two-thirds of sites not including such elements, even the sites with return visit elements do not appear to cater to journalists...

The findings suggest the need to post press releases regularly, organize appropriate materials in an online press room, post policy papers and statements, and identify specialists or experts and make them available to the press. Large national or international organizations are likely better at using their websites for press relations than are small, local, or regional grassroots organizations. But much activism occurs at the local level, so enhancing the ability of small activist organizations to provide useful information to journalists is essential.

In other words, the bad news is that most activism websites aren't useful to journalists—but the good news is that making your activism website useful to journalists isn't very difficult and could pay off.

Journalists need the following:

- **Something on deadline**—If journalists contact you, that usually means they're working on an article that they need to finish that afternoon, and they need a quote from somebody to represent your organization's point of view. Sometimes they also need statistical data: How many times have you read a feature that begins, "According to [group], [percent]% of..."? Or they need to cite a policy paper.

- **Accurate information**—All activism is biased, obviously, but that doesn't mean it has to be dishonest. Don't misrepresent the facts. If a journalist catches you in a lie or catches your website in a lie, that person will be reluctant to rely on you for quotes again.

- **Material organized in a way that media can really use**—It isn't a bad idea to create a press page or media room that's slightly busier than your supporter-targeted pages (journalists are accustomed to sifting through high word count pages to find what they need) and that includes in one place the information they need. This page is what Reber and Kim referred to as a "press room."

Let's look at a couple of online activist press rooms that do follow the Reber-Kim guidelines.

Case Study: The National Organization for Women (www.now.org)

This page (shown in Figure 3.9) holds 12 items, and they're all items that journalists can use. Note, in particular, the link to press releases—if your organization puts out press releases, make sure you keep an archive of them and link to them in one place—and the biographical information on officers.

You've probably noticed that for most of this chapter, I've emphasized content other than biographical and organizational material—local sites emphasizing events and local issues and national sites emphasizing donations, newsletters, and action alerts. For media, turn this on its head: They mainly want to know about you and your organization, and they're going to be less interested in opportunities to get involved because they don't really want to get involved. They just have to finish a story on deadline, and they're looking for sources and data.

NOW doesn't use this page as an opportunity to get journalists to attend one of their events or get involved in one of their action alert campaigns, and this is a good thing because that's not why journalists are looking at their site in the first place.

If your organization puts out press releases, Now's site is a fantastic example to emulate. But if it doesn't, or if you don't want to emphasize press releases, no worries. You can use other approaches to the press room, and Equality California's is compelling.

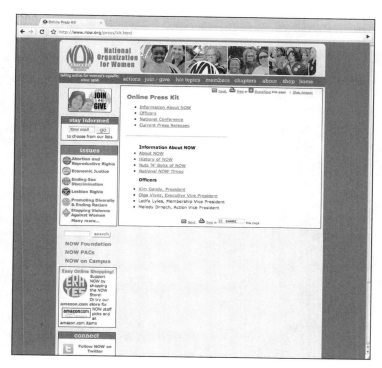

Figure 3.9

Press Kit page for the National Organization for Women (NOW).

Case Study: Equality California (http://www.eqca.org)

Three publications. Legislator data. Staff photos and bios. And that's it. Nothing much to say about the organization, how it's structured, or what its history is, and no links to press releases. So is the approach used by Equality California (shown in Figure 3.10) better or worse than the approach used by NOW?

Both. The simplicity is a plus, as is the emphasis on staff bios (journalists primarily need quotes), and easy access to three publications (the fact that only three are listed, and none of them are terribly long, helps). And I believe the importance of press releases is overrated. When I attended an activism and media conference earlier this year, speakers repeatedly emphasized that shorter press advisories generally work just as well and because newspapers aren't going to reprint press releases verbatim anyway.

But if you produce press releases, it's really a good idea to link them—especially the recent ones.

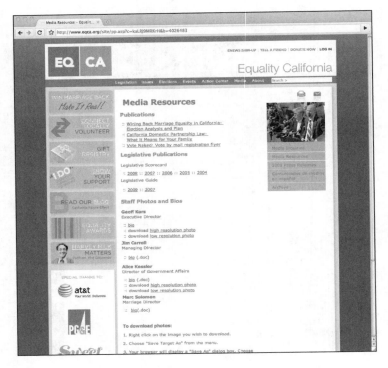

Figure 3.10
Media page of Equality California (EQCA).

Being Found

Okay, so you've created a website that targets your intended audience(s). Now what?

There are various studies on what percentage of a site's hits come from what sources. None of these studies focus on activism websites, so we'll completely ignore them here and use our common sense instead.

Generally speaking, your traffic will come from one or more of the following places.

Search Engines

Search engines are the primary referrers for nonlocal sites, as a general rule, and are well worth paying attention to, even for local sites. The most popular search engine (by far) is Google, so we'll focus on it—but the strategies you use to get your site found in Google will generally be applicable to other search engines as well.

The science of getting your site found by Google and other search engines is known as Search Engine Optimization (SEO), and entire books are dedicated to the topic. Que has published one, Rebecca Lieb's *The Truth About Search Engine Optimization*, which features 51 tips to get your site noticed by search engines.

Here are the basics:

- If your site is new, prepare to wait a while. It can take Google months to notice a new website.

- Every time you write a new page that specifically addresses something people are likely to search for, associate it with a keyword phrase. This isn't necessary if you're doing, for instance, an About Us page for your organization. But if you're active on animal rights issues and have done a page on dogfighting laws in Missouri, for example, be sure to use the words "dogfighting" and "Missouri" in your title and at least a few times in the article itself.

- If you're not sure which keywords to use, use a free keyword suggester service. Google AdWords has a free keyword suggestion tool (https://adwords.google.com/select/KeywordToolExternal), as does WordTracker (http://freekeywords.wordtracker.com/).

- Get legitimate cross-links. If other real sites cross-link your content, that tends to make it appear higher on the list of matches returned by Google and other search engines.

- Avoid scammy cross-links that charge money in exchange for free crosslinks. If link farms cross-link your content with specific intent to raise your rank in search engines, Google will tend to lower your rank when it finds out what's going on.

Cross-Links

If your site is new, you're probably going to rely almost exclusively on cross-links for your hits because you won't have had a chance to make it to the search engines. Asking for cross-links can be tricky, as I explain in Chapter 5.

Repeat Visitors

This is the best kind of traffic to get—users who keep returning to your site because they want to know what your organization is doing next. Most of the more popular ways of doing this—blogging, Twittering, or using newsletters for new content—are covered in Chapter 8.

Social Networking

If you set up a group on Facebook or MySpace to publicize new content on your website, that's a great way to give supporters a way to know when new content is online. For more on social networking, see Chapter 4.

Print

You can get a small amount of web traffic just by putting the URL on business cards, stationery, and flyers—and the more memorable it is, the better.

Word of Mouth

Every organization, no matter how big or how small, craves word-of-mouth advertising because it's the best kind to have. It comes with more credibility than anything else does, and it's based on real social connections—the kind that social networking only provides a medium for.

The best way to get word-of-mouth advertising? Create a really, really good site that people can't help talking about. This doesn't necessarily mean a fancy site, an expensive site, or a site you've sweated blood to create. More often it means a new idea, a new angle, or just being a big fish in a small pond. Your site doesn't have to be arterial, but it has to represent a new branch of some kind, a new capillary, a new strand. It has to mean something, and it has to mean something new.

Five Steps to Building a Great Activism Website

Want a great website? Here are five things you can do that tend to turn out, well, pretty great:

- Keep the focus on the people who are actually viewing the site. This may seem obvious, but a lot of people write activist websites with an eye for looking good, or to impress (or pacify) a few specific individuals in the organization or, in some cases, without trying to appeal to anyone at all—just following a rote pattern so they can say they put a website together. If you want a website that works, always try to consider it from the point of view of the people who will be looking at it.

- Keep it simple. You don't need to introduce a lot of unnecessary elaborate technologies into the website just to keep up with the Joneses. Sometimes simple is best. A good principle of web design: never provide your visitors with more options than they will actually want to use.

- Don't build what you can't maintain. Start small and build up from there after you've gotten the basics down to a science. If you're going to have a blog, don't just start one up, blog on it a few times, and then abandon it—that makes the site, cause, or organization look like it has been abandoned. If you're going to have a local calendar of events (I'll show you how to make one in Chapter 8), keep it up-to-date or don't bother. Fix broken links as you find them. This may sound like a lot of work, but it's a lot less work than scrambling to try to keep up with unrealistic expectations that you've set for yourself.

- Don't make a sales pitch. Many websites try to promote the organization as if it were a product, singing its praises and asking for donations. I don't know if this strategy technically results in more donations—my guess would be that it does not—but in any case, it's an impediment to using the site as an online organizing tool.

- Don't expect too much. In the end, your website doesn't have to be perfect. It just has to give visitors a reason to show up.

Your E-Activism Toolkit: Building a Website

> ## Your E-Activism Toolkit
> √ Getting Informed
> √ Planning a Web Site
> ☐ Social Networking
> ☐ Following the Rules
> ☐ Raising Money
> ☐ Using Multimedia
> ☐ Keeping Allies in the Loop
> ☐ Spreading Action Alerts and Petitions

So you've got your website up, and that's the stereotypical first step of any online activism endeavor. Can't do much without a website.

But what can you do with one?

In the previous chapter, you learned how to research information online. Now you've learned how your organization, cause, or initiative can be part of the information that other people research. You've put your organization's flag out there on the landscape, put your organization's handprints in the wet cement, and you're generally part of the Internet that other people experience. This is essential. It can't be understated.

Organizations overemphasize websites, no question. They might shell out $500 for a freelance web guru to put one together and then let it slide from there because they figure that's all there is to online activism. It isn't. It's just something you can use to anchor your other online activism.

For example:

- A website can give you a place to syndicate RSS feeds from the kinds of news sites I describe in Chapter 2.

- A website can provide links to groups and pages you've created on Facebook, MySpace, and other social networking sites I describe in Chapter 4.

- A website can give you a donation link that you can use to raise funds, as I describe in Chapter 6.

- A website can embed photographs, audio podcasts, and streaming video, as I describe in Chapter 7.

- A website can provide access to email newsletters, online calendars, mailing lists, Twitter feeds, and other online stay-up-to-date technologies I describe in Chapter 8.

- A website can provide access to action alerts and e-petitions, as I describe in Chapter 9.

- A website is like a coat rack: It's useful primarily because you can hang stuff on it. Content is king. And without that content, a website—like an empty coat rack—is just decoration. In and of itself, it doesn't build community.

One thing that does build community, though, is social networking. In the next chapter, I describe some ways that you can use social networking to augment your website.

Engage with Social Networking Sites

Leopold's Records was a fixture of Berkeley life for decades. Founded in 1968 by students at the University of California as a tribute to the conductor Leopold Stokowski, it wasn't just a record store—it was a center of the community. It also became, in 1972, the first real example of electronic social networking (and was often used to organize the sort of protests shown in Figure 4.1).

It began with a bulletin board, where people in the community stuck notes with for-sale notices, or advertisements, or just personal statements—essentially a primitive form of Craigslist. But in 1972, students rigged a computer terminal next to the bulletin board where people could sit down to read and write the same sorts of messages electronically. The terminal, called Community Memory, was the world's first bulletin board system (BBS).

Figure 4.1
The city of Berkeley, California has long been associated with traditional activism, but it was also home to the first electronic community social networking center. Photo: © 2008 John Martinez Pavliga. Licensed under Creative Commons (attribution license).

Later, most BBSs were configured to allow users to dial-up on modems. Before long, BBS operators got the idea to link BBSs together so that they would automatically call each other to share, and synchronize, topic-specific message databases called "echoes." Although BBSs would later offer other services, such as file downloading and online games, the basic bulletin board function of the BBS—in other words, social networking—remained central. When BBSs were largely replaced by the Internet in the early 1990s, it represented a tradeoff—users could take advantage of superior technology that would allow them to access a world full of information instantly, but the small community atmosphere of BBSs was gone.

Fortunately, new Internet social networking sites have created new ways to connect people, helping to bring back some of the community spirit that was lost in the transition between BBSs and the Internet. And much like the original Community Memory, which helped student activists at Berkeley organize and stay in contact, the new social networking technologies can help activists change the world.

Social Networking 101

Social networking sites are diverse, but most of them have the following features in common:

- **Profiles**—Users create special pages for themselves, allowing other users to read what they want to say. Example: My Facebook page lists my work history, educational background, favorite quotations, and so on. Users can also use profile pages to post blog entries or links to offsite content.

- **Friends**—Users can "friend" each other, creating links between their respective profiles and allowing them to more easily communicate. Example: I currently have 1,321 "friends" on Facebook—mostly people local to me—and all of them are updated whenever I make changes to my profile, post a link to content, or distribute a message.

- **Groups**—Users who don't know each other but have common interests can create online groups and then use the groups to distribute information to members. Example: I created a Facebook group for Crouzon Syndrome, a rare congenital medical condition that I inherited. Other Facebook users who have Crouzon Syndrome, or have children with Crouzon Syndrome, searched Facebook for relevant groups and found mine. Now it has 45 members.

Specific social networks have other features, but these three essentially define social networks as they currently exist. They're simple ideas, simple features, but implementing them on a large-scale basis creates unprecedented opportunities for online community organizing.

SOCIAL NETWORKING HAZARDS TO AVOID

When it's done right, social networking can be great for activism. When it's done badly, it can be an unwelcome distraction. Here are a few occupational hazards that come with using online social networking as part of your activism repertoire:

Problem: Time wasting—Some studies indicate that social networking decreases on-the-job productivity, and other studies indicate that it increases on-the-job productivity. Here's my guess: It increases productivity when you use it well and decreases productivity when you use it badly.

Solution: Be conscious of what you're doing—There's nothing intrinsically wrong with playing around on social networks; it's much healthier, more fun, and more productive than watching television. But if you're about to put in some time building activism on social networks, don't let yourself get distracted by other stuff until you're certain you want to take a break.

Problem: Harassment—If you take on a controversial cause, some people will probably object and will try to derail your group by making inappropriate posts, or harassing members, or otherwise causing trouble.

Solution: Tattle—Social networking sites have terms of service agreements that prohibit inappropriate behavior. If the behavior is threatening in nature, you can—and generally should—also report it to law enforcement.

Problem: Spammers—Some social networking sites are overrun by people trying to sell you stuff (or trick you into falling for a scam), and they're all fighting for your time and attention.

Solution: Lock the door—Most social networking sites have optional privacy features that you can use to reduce the amount of spam traffic. If you're getting too many spammy Add Friend requests on MySpace, for example, enable the feature that requires anyone who attempts to add your profile to their friends list to retype a string of nonmachine-readable text to prove they're not automated spamming software.

Facebook

http://www.facebook.com

The world's largest active Internet social networking site could also probably be characterized as the most useful social networking site, by far, for most activists. If you do activism through only one social networking site, make it Facebook. Why? Because Facebook is...

- **Big**—And I mean really big, with over 300 million active users.

- **Personal**—Whereas MySpace and other networks are based on a culture of anonymity, which makes most people difficult to find, Facebook is based on a culture of real names and real locations. This makes it easy to cross-check Facebook content with phone trees and paper mailing lists to determine who does and doesn't have access to a bulletin you might have posted to other Facebook users or to search Facebook for local activists you already know offline.

- **Event friendly**—Facebook allows you to promote events online, giving friends, local group members, or members of the general public (your choice) the opportunity to receive invitations to specific events and RSVP to indicate whether they are likely to attend. Afterward, you can upload digital photos of the event to Facebook and tell supporters how it went.

- **Privacy conscious**—You can edit your profile to make specific material available only to specific users. For example, you could post a photo album that only officers in your organization can see.

- **Full-featured**—Facebook's feature set is large and grows every day, and tens of thousands of user-supported add-on applications expand its functionality even further.

In other words, Facebook is huge and popular for a reason. There's a small learning curve involved before you can get used to the more advanced features, but once you're there, you're there. Facebook can be one of the most effective online organizing tools you'll ever use.

CAUSES: A FACEBOOK APPLICATION WORTH USING

Facebook applications tend to be—let's face it—mindlessly entertaining at best. But some serve a really useful function, including one specifically geared toward activism.

Causes (http://apps.facebook.com/causes/), maintained by Project Agape, allows users to state their support for organizations in a public way, recruit new supporters, and even pledge to raise funds or increase membership—and to compete for top spots in these categories. It's arguably a must-have for any Facebook-engaged activist organization.

Facebook Case Study: The Obama Campaign

It's impossible to know exactly how much of an impact Facebook had on the success of Barack Obama's 2008 presidential campaign, but it certainly had an impact on its grassroots character (see Figure 4.2). And no example better illustrates this than Students for Barack Obama.

Students for Barack Obama was created as a Facebook group in July 2006 by Meredith Segal, a student at Bowdoin College. By the time Obama officially announced his candidacy six months later, it had already accumulated over 50,000 members—and would eventually attract over 250,000 members. Students for Barack Obama would later become the official student outreach wing of the Obama campaign, and Segal brought in to direct it. The Facebook group is still in effect after Obama's victory and will presumably remain so through the 2012 reelection campaign.

Figure 4.2
Barack Obama, still running for president at the time, addresses the Netroots Nation conference in July 2008. Online activism played a more significant role in the Obama campaign than in any other major-party presidential campaign in U.S. history. Photo: © 2008 Neeta Lind. Licensed under Creative Commons (attribution license).

The Obama campaign also established an official page for the candidate, which accumulated over 5 million members by February 2009.

The Obama campaign's outreach to Facebook was not limited to grassroots organizing. In March 2007, the campaign tapped Facebook cofounder Chris Hughes to work full-time to create MyBarackObama, a social networking site tailored specifically to the needs of the Obama campaign. The site networked more than 2 million Obama volunteers, donors, and supporters to create what can be described, without hyperbole, as the largest and most efficient organized phone-banking initiative in the history of American politics.

MySpace

http://www.myspace.com

If Facebook is the brash new king of social networking, MySpace is the lion in winter. But with "only" 125 million users (it's not clear exactly how many of them are active), it's still enormous. And MySpace offers some features that Facebook does not currently offer. Most notably, Facebook does not offer customizable profiles that can be tailored to meet the needs of specific users or activist organizations. What's more, MySpace—despite being smaller than Facebook—makes more money per pageview because of the site's ad-heavy layout, ensuring its financial viability for the foreseeable future.

MySpace is also notable for the way it handles music. Users can customize their profiles with (legally licensed) theme songs. My profile, for example, currently greets users with Nikka Costa's "Everybody Got Their Something" and then moves through a series of other tracks before concluding with Phil Ochs' somber existential ballad "When I'm Gone." This works for organizations, too, so your urban poverty relief organization can use Marvin Gaye's "Inner City Blues (Makes Me Wanna Holler)," your feminist organization can use Le Tigre's "New Kicks," or your antiwar organization can use U2's "Peace on Earth." The possibilities are overwhelmingly numerous.

But for all its advantages vis-a-vís presentation, MySpace is not quite as social as Facebook, at least not yet. Its handling of events means that it's much harder to handle invites and RSVP on MySpace, as it presently stands. It also relies on aliases rather than real names, with no associated regional or business networks (and limited search capabilities), which can make it impossible to find your friends and allies. And some progressive activists also take issue with the fact that MySpace is a subsidiary of Rupert Murdoch's notoriously conservative News Corporation, which owns FOX News, *The Wall Street Journal*, the *New York Post*, and the *Weekly Standard*.

It makes practical sense to set up an organizational page on MySpace and customize it reasonably well, but odds are you'll find yourself using it a lot less often than you use your organizational page on Facebook.

Other Social Networking Sites

Facebook and MySpace are the biggest social networking sites, but they're not the *only* social networking sites—and sometimes a smaller, more specialized site is exactly what you need.

- **Ning**—www.ning.com—Ning isn't so much a single social networking site as a database that allows users to create their own social networks, but this comes with its own set of practical advantages. First, organizations can limit themselves to a self-contained database of users, which is useful if you want to create a small-scale social network that includes only the people you want to include. Second, it's extremely customizable, allowing you to design the entire format of the site around your organization's priorities. Third, its event features, with invites and RSVPs, are very sophisticated. Its event features are arguably the strongest of any social networking site other than Facebook. If you're dealing with a small group of volunteers who won't mind writing new profiles from scratch just for your site, Ning could be exactly what you need.

- **Twitter**—www.twitter.com—I discuss Twitter in more detail in Chapter 8, but it's worth mentioning that in addition to its news distribution options (which define it), Twitter is a full-fledged social networking site (albeit based on "followers"/"followees" rather than reciprocal friends).

- **Idealist.org**—www.idealist.org—Idealist.org isn't *exactly* a social networking site. It's more of a combination social networking site, information center, and bulletin board for jobs and volunteer opportunities. Its database includes (as of press time) a mere 200,000 users and 85,000 organizations, which is infinitesimally small compared to the massive, triple-digit-million sized databases you can find on Facebook and MySpace. But it has all of the features that make a social networking site unique, and it's specifically targeted to people who work and play in the nonprofit sector, so it's well worth looking into for that reason.

- **Friendster**—www.friendster.com—Friendster was the first big social networking site. Though it has been eclipsed by Facebook and MySpace, it still boasts 90 million active users and could be a useful place for your organization to plant a flag if you want to maximize your social networking options.

- **Orkut**—www.orkut.com—You would think that a social network owned by Google would dominate the field, but Orkut has been a surprisingly quiet player in the United States—though it has caught on in India and Brazil (most of its users come from Asia and Latin America), and its simple layout is perfect for low-bandwidth connections. If your organization focuses on international issues, Orkut could be worth your time. If it's strictly U.S. focused, it might not be.

- **CommunityConnect—BlackPlanet/MiGente/AsianAve**—www.blackplanet.com, www.migente.com, www.asianave.com—These sites specifically target ethnic audiences—African-American, Latino, and Asian-American, respectively—and boast some 20 million active users. But the software used to operate these sites is not particularly fun to use, and finding specific users can be challenging given the limited search options. Radio One purchased the sites for $38 million in 2008, which may lead to some improvements in the interface.

- **LinkedIn**—LinkedIn is extremely popular and growing rapidly in size, but it's more of a résumé-sharing site with social networking features than a social networking site in the traditional sense. It's a great site to use if you're looking for activism jobs or want to network with other up-and-coming professional activists, but it's less useful as a venue for activism itself.

Summary: Social Networking

In the last two chapters, you learned how to use the Web to find information and how to use the Web to be found. You might find yourself wondering why social networking is such a big deal right now. Aren't we basically talking about more websites and more ways to search websites?

Well, yes and no. Social networking is more like *online dating*, if you'll pardon the comparison: You get on it to meet and interact with other people. People hear about websites through Google. But people will hear about your social networking pages through their friends on the social networking sites, and this will color the way they interact with it and what they expect to see from it.

Your E-Activism Toolkit

- [ ] Getting Informed
- [ ] Building a Web Site
- [ ] Social Networking
- [ ] Following the Rules
- [ ] Raising Money
- [ ] Using Multimedia
- [ ] Keeping Allies in the Loop
- [ ] Spreading Action Alerts and Petitions

Let's say you've done everything else I've described in this book up to this point—you've figured out what else is out there, set up a website for your particular flavor of e-activism to fill in the gap, and now you're investigating Facebook. What Facebook (and other state-of-the-art social networking sites) have to offer that your existing website doesn't is

- **A sense of community**—People actually *join* your Facebook group, at which point they will receive regular updates alongside updates from other groups. They can communicate with other friends who belong to your group. Their profiles, privacy settings permitting, advertise that they are members of your cause's Facebook group. Your Facebook group brings you into direct contact with your supporters; rather than passively receiving information from you, they are part of an online community.

- **Decent event planning**—Let's say you're planning a protest in two weeks. If you're sticking it up on your website, good luck—how many people are likely to read it within the next two weeks, much less remember it in time to attend? But Facebook lets them RSVP yes or maybe and then provides them with reminders up to and including the day of the event. This RSVP feature also gives you some indication of how many people might be planning to attend.

- **Simple access to media**—Chapter 7 tells you how to use some of the more focused Internet multimedia sites out there, but Facebook and MySpace have their own photo- and video-hosting features. This lets you both plan events and provide your own coverage of events to members of the group.

- **The fun factor**—Social networking sites are designed to be *fun to use*. For my part, I send more Facebook messages than I do emails these days—Facebook's interface is just easier and more pleasant to work with.

If you're putting your cause online, one of the most effective things you can do is set up and properly promote a Facebook group page for your organization or cause. And if you're wondering what constitutes *proper* promotion, keep reading, my friends. In the next chapter, we're talking about netiquette.

A Short Guide to the Ethics and Etiquette of Online Activism

"Tradition is a guide and not a jailer."

—W. Somerset Maugham

If you want to see a great exercise in applied moral philosophy, get your hands on a copy of Saul Alinsky's *Rules for Radicals*. Published in 1971 to help young community organizers do their jobs in a way that actually gets stuff done, rather than in a way that simply makes them feel better about themselves, Alinsky's little book is one of the wisest I've ever read. You'll probably love parts of it and hate parts of it, and that's really kind of the point, but you'll learn from it. And after you've read it once, you'll probably reread it.

I don't want to just paraphrase his second chapter, titled "Of Means and Ends," which deals in general terms with the same sorts of ideas we discuss in this chapter. And I don't want to get way off topic and go into any great detail about the field of moral philosophy or what it means to be an ethical or good person—there are plenty of books about that, most of them useless for our purposes. But I'd like to talk a little bit about a point he makes regarding means and ends because I think it's important to this chapter. He writes:

> The organizer, the revolutionist, the activist or call him what you will, who is committed to free and open society is in that commitment anchored to a complex of high values...These values include freedom, equality, justice, peace, the right to dissent; the values that were the banners of hope and learning of all revolutions...

> Means and ends are so qualitatively interrelated that the true question has never been the proverbial one, "Does the End justify the Means?," but always has been "Does this *particular* end justify this *particular* means?"

This is important. Alinsky brings up the example of terrorism—fighting a government by taking civilian hostages and blowing stuff (and people) up is always wrong, right? Well, Mahatma Gandhi (see Figure 5.1)—arguably the most effective activist of the twentieth century—thought so. But for the partisans who violently resisted the Nazis during World War II, partisans who would not have been able to do so by less radical means, violence was essential. Or we can look at Abraham Lincoln's pre-abolitionist argument that no state should or may secede against the United States because "a house divided against itself cannot stand." Wouldn't King George have been able to make the same argument prior to the American Revolution? (President Lincoln was in a much stronger position, morally, after he issued the Emancipation Proclamation and made abolition of slavery a clear part of the Union cause.)

Figure 5.1
What makes Mahatma Gandhi's philosophy of passive resistance effective in most contexts is not its moral purity, but rather its efficacy. Even Martin Luther King Jr., Gandhi's most prominent ideological heir, did not fully support passive resistance until it was proven effective during the Montgomery Bus Boycott. Photo: Public domain.

Alinsky recommends looking at your options before you choose a strategy and then going with the options that are (a) least morally objectionable among the available options and (b) most likely to work. In a practical sense, (b) implies (a) anyway. For example, terrorism *doesn't* usually work—especially in a democracy, where public outrage over terrorism will generally promote a policy agenda contrary to whatever it is the terrorists want. Hawkish leaders in the United States successfully waged two elective wars after the 9/11 attacks, something that would have been unthinkable beforehand, and instituted the most aggressive assassination program in U.S. history against terrorist leaders. All in all, that was a pretty lousy deal for both al-Qaeda and their agenda—even before we bring morality into the picture. Likewise, the violence initiated by certain segments of the anti-abortion movement during the 1990s effectively took the idea of a national abortion ban off the table and may have done so permanently. In a democratic system, being a nut isn't only unnecessary—it's destructive to your cause.

In this chapter, we talk about the seven deadly sins of online activism. There are moral arguments that can probably be made against each of them, but for purposes of this book I'm mostly interested in the fact that in addition to being unethical and rude, these strategies just don't work.

Deadly Sin #1: Self-Promotion at the Expense of the Movement

Every time I write an activism-focused bio, I feel a little bit like Daffy Duck. You might know what I'm talking about: the old Looney Tunes shorts where Daffy fights with Bugs Bunny or Porky Pig to make sure he gets the credit he thinks he deserves. Those cartoons weren't originally made for kids, and the older I get, the more I get the subtext. We're all a little bit like Daffy Duck, some more than others.

The activist world is a lousy way to manifest that tendency. Now, I'm not saying that you can't or shouldn't promote yourself and that you should let other people take credit for your work. And I'm not saying that there can't even be a place in the movement for personalities. Martin Luther King, Jr. did a lot of self-promotion, as did Mohandas Gandhi, as did Cesar Chavez, as did Betty Friedan, and the list goes on and on. We've heard of these people, in most cases, because they did a certain amount of self-promotion. If they worked silently and invisibly and let any random idiot take the credit for what they did, they never would have been able to put themselves in a position where they could steer their movements and accomplish the things they accomplished. So I'm not knocking self-promotion. It has its place.

But that place isn't center stage.

For every Deadly Sin in this chapter, you could mentally insert the phrase "at the Expense of the Movement." So the question with online activism, as with other forms of activism, is: What do you think you're doing? Why are you doing this? Who will this help or hurt? (This question is often asked of PETA, as explained in Figure 5.2.)

For example, if someone goes to the organization's website and sees a great big photo of *you* and a bio associated with it, what message does that send? Maybe it sends a very good message; the Children's Defense Fund benefits when it highlights Marian Wright Edelman's name because she has so much clout and so much history and is so well-known. And the Muscular Dystrophy Association benefits tremendously, in terms of both branding and popularity, by its association with Jerry Lewis. Charlton Heston did incredible good for the cause of gun rights by promoting himself as president of the National Rifle Association. Nobody could accuse any of these three people of *excessive* self-promotion because their self-promotion actually worked; it benefited their respective movements.

Figure 5.2

PETA's protests often involve nudity, violent imagery, and other controversial content, as shown in this antifur protest. Although PETA's work unquestionably brings more attention to the organization, whether it does so in a manner that is ultimately beneficial to the cause of animal rights is a frequently debated question. Photo: Copyright 2007 SVTCobra (Wikinews contributor). Licensed under Creative Commons Attribution License 2.5.

Does your self-promotion benefit your movement or cause? That's a good question to ask yourself as you design a website, a social networking group, or something else and decide how much of it is going to be about *you* and other prominent volunteers. It can be helpful to put a human face on things—email updates should always come from a person *at* an organization, for example, and not from the faceless organization. (More on this in Chapter 8.) And it's good if people can associate an organization with specific personalities. But it's more necessary in activism than it is in most other areas of life to ask: Am I doing this for *me* (and/or the prestige of my organization), or am I doing this for what I believe in?

Deadly Sin #2: Unsolicited Bulk Email

This is more of a hypothetical sin than something online activists actually *do,* but there are good reasons why it isn't being done and good reasons why you shouldn't try it.

If you've ever watched *South Park*, you probably know the hilariously inept school counselor, Mr. Mackey, from his catchphrase: "Drugs are bad, mmkay?" This is not a "spam is bad, mmkay?" section. There are specific reasons why bulk-mailing total strangers to promote your cause is a really bad idea, potentially relevant issues of criminal and civil law aside:

- **It makes you look desperate**—Spamming is to community organizing what proposing marriage on a first date is to your love life. it sends the message that you have nothing to offer (or something to hide).

- **It annoys people**—'Nuff said.

- **People don't read it**—Over 100 billion spam messages are sent each day, but only 12% of Internet users have ever clicked on a spam URL with the intention of possibly taking advantage of the spammer's offer.

If you find yourself eyeing an ad from a general bulk emailing service and wondering if this might be a useful approach to try…no. It isn't. Use targeted email distribution lists, which I describe in Chapter 8, instead—and send messages that focus on your target group, that don't annoy people (or that at least annoy people less), and stand a much better chance of actually getting read.

Deadly Sin #3: Hacktivism

In 2004, a small group of pro-Democratic activists had an idea: Why not get a bunch of users together to simultaneously load up Republican web servers at a specific time, overwhelming them? Ignoring basic questions of the law (this technique, known as a denial-of-service attack, is illegal in some jurisdictions), this is a potentially harmful, and in most contexts ultimately ineffective, strategy. I'll explain why in a moment—but first, a little history.

The first recorded semi-successful "hacktivism" incident was the Worms Against Nuclear Killers (WANK) worm, launched by Australian hackers against NASA's computers on October 16th, 1989, in ostensible protest against alleged radioactive danger associated with the Galileo probe (see Figure 5.3). Worms aren't the threat to Internet security that they used to be, but the time was when they were scary beasts. As cybercrime historian Suelette Dreyfus puts it:

> A computer worm is a little like a computer virus. It invades computer systems, interfering with their normal functions. It travels along any available compatible computer network and stops to knock at the door of systems attached to that network. If there is a hole in the security of the computer system, it will crawl through and enter the system. When it does this, it might have instructions to do any number of things, from sending computer users a message to trying to take over the system. What makes a worm different from other computer programs, such as viruses, is that it is self-propagating. It propels itself forward, wiggles into a new system and propagates itself at the new site. Unlike a virus, a worm doesn't latch onto a data file or a program. It is autonomous.

> > > **NOTE**

Read more about the history of cybercrime here: Suelette Dreyfus and Julian Assange, *Underground: Hacking, Madness, and Obsession on the Electronic Frontier*, Kew: Random House Australia, 2001. Online edition. URL: www.xs4all.nl/~suelette/underground/justin/contents.html.

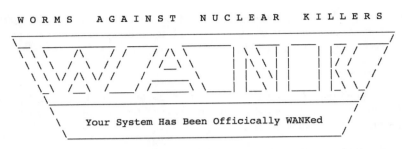

You talk of times of peace for all, and then prepare for war.

Figure 5.3
This appeared on the screens of NASA employees on October 16th, 1989. Public domain image, courtesy of the National Aeronautics and Space Administration (NASA).

An Anti-Nuclear Message

The quote shown in Figure 5.3 ("You talk of times of peace for all, and then prepare for war.") is from Midnight Oil's "(The City of) Blossom and Blood," off their *Species and Deceases* (1985) album. The full stanza reads:

You the warriors with your words,
throw away your spears.
You talk of times of peace for all
and then prepare for war.

The eponymous city of blossom and blood is Hiroshima, Japan, which was attacked in the world's first nuclear strike by the United States on August 6, 1945.

In this case, the WANK worm took over NASA computers intermittently for two weeks and printed fake text on the screen that led users to believe that their files—often sensitive research files—had been deleted. While the worm didn't disrupt the launch of the Galileo probe, it caused a serious headache for NASA's computing staff.

There have been many defensible examples of benevolent hacktivism—most notably, hacktivism directed against government programs restricting Internet access in China and Iran. But hacktivism is ultimately about three components: skilled programmers, adequate access, and adequate bandwidth. And *all three components can be purchased*. None of these components necessitates a movement. In the long run, the propagation of hacktivism—and its widespread use and acceptance—would allow those with the most money to make unlimited use of it, whereas grassroots movements would be left with a disadvantage. Hacktivism can literally be bought, with no community support whatsoever.

In other words, community activists who contribute to the spread of hacktivism contribute to the spread of a new online activism where community activism matters less and government or megacorporate sponsorship matters more. We don't really want hacktivism to catch on; in the long run, that would work against us.

Besides, it doesn't usually work out so well anyway. That effort by pro-Democratic activists to shut down Republican websites? It didn't have any real effect on the election. If the approximately 40,000 participants each donated 20 bucks to a specific local race instead, the extra $800,000 probably would have made more of an impact. And if they didn't want to give money, having 40,000 volunteers on a phone bank isn't anything to sneeze at, either.

Deadly Sin #4: Violating Copyright

Unlike spam and hacktivism, copyright violations are endemic in online activism. Some people even believe that if copyrighted material is redistributed by a nonprofit organization, the organization is automatically shielded from liability. I'm not an attorney, but I know this isn't true.

I can think of three very good reasons why redistributing copyrighted material that you haven't been given permission to redistribute, as part of an activism initiative, is a bad idea:

1. It can get you sued.

2. It makes you look sloppy.

3. Have I mentioned that it can get you sued?

In Chapter 7, I explain how to find copylefted and public domain material that you can use in your activism efforts. That's a much safer, and therefore more useful, approach than just cutting-and-pasting something from a website.

> > > **NOTE**

Not all copyrighted material is out of bounds! Some copyright owners deliberately "copyleft" their content by copyrighting it with a license that allows for free redistribution at no cost and without permission.

Deadly Sin #5: Nagging

A local activist gave me a piece of advice once: He always bulk-emails supporters about an event a month before it happens, then again two weeks before it happens, then a week before it happens, and then every day of the week up until the day it happens. Then he sends out one last invite two hours before the event happens and another update the next day announcing how great the event was.

Yeah, you probably shouldn't do that.

Online communication is the most convenient way to nag somebody. Unlike telephoning, it does not require one-on-one time—you can contact people in bulk. And unlike snail mail letters, postcards, and such, it costs nothing, arrives instantly, and does not require any real prep time. So the temptation is certainly there to bug people constantly, to keep your events and causes on their minds, and up to a certain point this is very beneficial to your cause. But there is a point of diminishing return.

Exactly how much nagging is too much? It's hard to say, which is why listening is important. If people who are participating in the organization—and I mean people who actually participate because anybody can sit on the sidelines and criticize—express concerns that they're receiving way too much email, it's probably best to back it down.

Tone is also important. People don't usually want to attend events that they associate with negative feelings and drama. If attendance at the last monthly meeting was lower than you think it should have been, berating your supporters *en masse* is a bad idea because they don't really owe you anything. It's not that they're not committed activists, necessarily, but people can choose many, many avenues to make the world a better place; why pick one that involves failure, shame, and verbal abuse? So be positive. As one old midrash tells us: "Angels do not lie, but neither are they stupid." Several years ago I organized a meeting for local writers at a coffee shop, and only six people showed up. I'd promoted the event online and was disappointed in the low turnout, but the way I described it was that the meeting was a success (which it was, given an appropriately scaled definition of success) and that we had difficulty finding enough seats to accommodate the number of people who showed (which we did because we were sitting on the patio and there was a concert inside). I'm not saying you should spin things *that* much, but what you say about an event—before and after—should ideally make people a little bit excited. It should make them want to show up to future events so they don't miss out on the experience.

If people are treated in a hostile way by a movement, it can create unintended side effects. Christopher Hitchens was regarded as a liberal, but the international Left's response to the 9/11 attacks—which sometimes vilified the United States, portraying it as a worthy target—made it easier for him to become a neoconservative. And Rep. Michelle Bachmann (R-MN), a leader in the American conservative movement, was a nominal Democrat until a passage in a Gore Vidal book, criticizing the Founding Fathers, made her question her party's commitment to classical liberal philosophy. This shouldn't inspire anyone to be more centrist or moderate than they are in their personal beliefs—people should speak what they consider to be the truth without fear that it might turn others off—but when you're doing activism, it pays to be strategic and think of how your audience is likely to react. If the gut-level impression you give potential supporters is that you're angry and negative, it will almost certainly make them less likely to take your cause seriously.

Deadly Sin #6: Violating Privacy

Online media is all about distributing information, which can be very unpleasant if the information being distributed isn't intended for distribution.

Legal issues aside, it's usually a bad idea to distribute private emails, contact information, and other material that the sender has not agreed, implicitly or explicitly, to let you distribute. It undermines trust in the organization, it contributes to burnout, and it generally drives people away. People like to be able to control access to their stories, their information, their identities, and if you deprive them of that control, they understandably tend to leave.

This isn't just theory. I can think of some real situations I've witnessed in recent years where people did not honor privacy and did real damage to their causes. Out of respect for the privacy of participants (see what I did there?), I haven't mentioned any names or identifying information:

- A local pastor deals with a dispute with a local church board member by secretly for-warding copies of the board member's private emails, which include material of an obviously confidential nature, to the congregational president. After discovering this, the board member suffers an instant case of burnout; he disappears from the congrega-tion within a year. The rest of the board is brought into the controversy and, within two years, the pastor and board president also leave the congregation.

- An officer in a nonprofit advocacy organization makes some suggestions regarding possible online activism content to the local president in a private email. The president replies to the email, sends copies to several other officers who were not originally on the recipient list, and mercilessly ridicules the suggestions.

- An organization decides to reward donors who have contributed more than $1,000 within the past year by honoring them by name in the online newsletter—without ask-ing their permission first. The wealthy donors are horrified to be named, working-class donors are horrified that their monetary sacrifices aren't given the same level of acknowledgment, and fundraising plummets the next year.

Violating privacy, like the other six Deadly Sins of online activism, is a bad idea primarily because it's destructive to your cause.

Deadly Sin #7: Being Scary

I'm going to step offline for a good example of this. Operation Save America, a conservative religious group, held its annual event in Jackson, Mississippi, in July 2006, sending hundreds of activists to picket the state's only remaining abortion clinic. I was among the local prochoice counterprotestors. It was, at the time, the largest activism event I had ever participated in.

Although I'm proud of the counterprotest in general, some people on both sides made major strategic errors. A few young folks who had come down to help decided to "mingle" with the Operation Save America people at their own events, sometimes in a disruptive way. On YouTube, there is a video of a young woman from this group screaming at length into the ear of a frightened-looking young man clutching a Bible. Who does this help?

But the biggest mistakes were on the other side. Fourteen of the anti-abortion protestors were arrested on various charges—no easy feat in a state as conservative as Mississippi. There was a bomb threat against prochoicers at the local state park. And, as the event wrapped up, some of the anti-abortion protestors decided to burn a Qur'an and a rainbow flag to state their opposition to Islam and homosexuality.

Yes, you read that right. At a national protest against an abortion clinic, they decided to burn a Qur'an and a rainbow flag.

This had a predictable effect: The church that had hosted their presence stated that they were no longer welcome to lodge there. Local Muslims, belonging to a religious community not generally associated with conspicuous support of abortion and gay rights, found unexpected allies. (The next week, a local imam preached the sermon at the city's liberal Unitarian Universalist church.) Members of the local gay rights community who had not previously had any interest in prochoice activism joined the counterprotestors. Operation Save America ended the week outnumbered, unwelcome, and humiliated.

Where did they fail? I'd argue that their *biggest* mistake was broadening their message to the point where instead of advocating a specific, sane-sounding point of view (namely, the view that fetuses are human beings and deserve legal protection), they advocated ideological warfare with huge swaths of the local community. They burned things in public, voraciously condemned large groups of people without much apparent forethought, and generally made locals uncomfortable. This marginalized them in a community that otherwise would have been receptive to their message.

Don't Be Creepy

Worried about scaring people? Here are five tips to bear in mind:

- **Avoid unnecessarily violent rhetoric of every kind**—Don't casually throw around metaphors that involve decapitation, evisceration, and so on. People visualize what you're reading, and if you can't discuss a policy issue without sounding like the script to a *Kill Bill* sequel, you're going to frighten potential allies away.

  The 2009 Tea Party protests, initially organized in response to the 2008-2009 U.S. government bailouts of the banking and insurance industries, were tainted by an attendance and a rhetoric that overlapped with the violent paramilitary "patriot" movement (as shown in Figure 5.4). If you talk about killing and murder and bloodshed, even if you're speaking metaphorically, people are probably going to want to back away slowly.

Figure 5.4
A Tea Party protester holds up a sign reading "I WILL GIVE MY BLOOD FOR MY CHILDRENS[sic] FREEDOM." Photo: © 2009 Street Protest TV via Flickr. Licensed under Creative Commons Attribution License 2.0 Generic.

- **Don't talk in a bigoted way about groups**—Even excessive, repetitive condemnation of your ideological opposition makes you sound more cranky than radical.

- **Don't focus on personalities**—If you keep mentioning someone, especially a local ideological opponent, by name, it comes across as if you're targeting that person in some way. Keep your focus on the change you're trying to achieve, not on the individuals who most prominently disagree with what you're advocating.

- **Promote your events, not the opposition's**—Occasionally you may find it necessary to counterprotest public events, but as a general rule anything you suggest that comes across as an invitation to disrupt other people's private or group activities will come across as creepy.

- **As much as possible, be positive and pragmatic**—The message you should be sending is one of achievable change, not unavoidable doom. Unavoidable doom isn't worth picketing. Avoidable doom is a much better target for your activism.

This applies to online activism, too. If you think 9/11 was a government conspiracy but your activism issue is abolition of the death penalty, don't mention the former opinion on the latter website. There's nothing wrong with being a committed member of an ideological minority group, but if you come across as being *against* people instead of *for* a specific policy change, you'll probably hurt your cause.

Your E-Activism Toolkit: Following the Rules

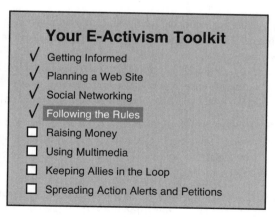

Having an ethics chapter in a book about activism is in some respects superfluous because every chapter in the book should reek of ethics and morality and decency and all that noble, wonderful stuff. And I think that's more or less true when we're talking about very specific issues—Chapter 7 deals with multimedia, for example, so that's the place to go if you're looking for hints about tagging people in photographs—but some general ethical principles echo throughout the book that are worth keeping in mind here.

If I were a real ethicist, a real moralist, the central message of this chapter would be "do unto others as you would have them do unto you." (I did, in fact, write Que Publishing's *The Absolute Beginner's Guide to the Bible*, published in 2005.) But this book is primarily about the *how* of changing the world, not the *why*, so the message is a little simpler: "Do unto others as is most likely to advance your cause, within reason."

It should go without saying that I'm not writing this book with white nationalists, violent international terrorists, and other perpetrators of human evil in mind, so I'm not writing this chapter for them. I'm writing this chapter for you, the well-meaning online activist, and this means that you already have a pretty good idea of what sort of behavior falls under the heading of "within reason" and what sort of behavior doesn't.

But we get distracted. In a very real sense, every human being who has ever lived has at least a mild case of attention-deficit disorder—because being able to control our focus is difficult. And this applies even to our moral focus.

So even good people can make the mistake of committing one of the previously described Deadly Sins. I've committed a few of them myself—activism is a great social outlet for me, for example, so I'm really bad about self-promotion. Other bolder, less egotistical people might need to be talked out of using hacktivism as a way to promote their causes.

On the face of it, that sounds silly—Patrick Henry didn't say, "Give me liberty or give me death, but I draw the line at appearing in public with my shoes unbuckled"—but when we're talking about behavior that is going to be detrimental to the causes we're fighting for, it makes sense to talk, in a general sense, about ethics and netiquette. So we've talked about it. Read, mark, and inwardly digest. And as we go through other kinds of activism, look at how the basic principles of this chapter might be relevant to them.

If you're designing a website, for example, Deadly Sin #1 is a serious risk—plenty of activism websites (I won't name names) are *all* about promoting the prestige of the organization rather than the cause, or even promoting the personality cult of an individual associated with it. And I do discuss this in a freestanding way in Chapter 3, but the basic principle of not promoting yourself or your group at the expense of your cause is crucial to online activism because it is *so easy* to make that mistake when you have a potential audience of near-unlimited size.

Email netiquette is discussed in greater depth in Chapter 8, which focuses on how we get people in the loop and keep them there, but Deadly Sin #2 is worth highlighting here because unsolicited bulk email is an idea that *sounds* worthwhile but isn't. Likewise hacktivism, Deadly Sin #3. The same could be said, really, of any item on this list.

Deadly Sins #5, #6, and #7—don't nag, don't violate privacy, don't use "terror-lite" techniques (even accidentally)—are all about not turning into the sorts of people who are detrimental to our cause. Because humanity is central to what we do as activists; because we need to maintain the ability to connect to people; because if we lose our humanity, scandals will follow us, and our movements will suffer as a result. Activism is one of the *very* few areas of life where being a good person and having noble priorities almost always pays off because activism attracts noble people and, online or offline, they can usually tell if you're faking it sooner or later.

How to Raise Funds Online

> "There is nothing quite as wonderful as money!
>
> There is nothing like a newly minted pound!
>
> Everyone must hanker
>
> for the butchness of a banker;
>
> it's accountancy that makes the world go round!"
>
> —Monty Python's Flying Circus, Episode 29

I t's possible to run an online activism initiative at little or no cost if you can secure free (or cheap) hosting and rely on volunteers for labor. If you're starting from scratch, and especially if you're working alone or with a small group of volunteers, that may be the best way to go about it.

But if you're setting up an online presence for an existing organization, it makes sense to accept donations online. As online politics guru Colin Delany explains:

> ...[I]t helps a campaign immensely if most individual donations, even the big ones, come in online rather than as paper checks. Money collected via credit cards is available instantly...Plus, online donation details automatically end up in a database, simplifying accounting and reporting... .

By contrast, physical checks present an immense logistical burden because each one has to be processed individually, whether it's collected at a fundraising dinner or arrives in the mail. It is for this reason that physical currency (shown in Figure 6.1) no longer plays a significant role in online fundraising.

Figure 6.1
In this 1904 photo, employees examine new paper currency minted by the U.S. Bureau of Engraving and Printing. Photo: Public domain. Image courtesy of the Library of Congress.

> > > N O T E

To learn more about online politics, see Colin Delany's, "Learning from Obama's Financial Steamroller: How to Raise Money Online." See www.epolitics.com/2009/05/15/learning-from-obamas-financial-steamroller-how-to-raise-money-online.

Asking for money in any medium (as shown in Figure 6.2) is an acquired skill; it doesn't come naturally to most people. If it feels a little awkward to you, no worries; it feels awkward to most people. (It does get easier over time.) If you're raising money for a cause, one important thing to remember, and to make supporters remember, is that the money is going somewhere—you're presumably not just hoarding it; it's not just going down a hole.

For example, here's how five prominent organizations ask for money:

- **ColorOfChange.org**

   https://secure.colorofchange.org/contribute/

   What It Says: "ColorOfChange.org is powered by YOU—your energy and dollars. We take no money from lobbyists or large corporations that don't share our values, and our tiny staff ensures your contributions go a long way. Every contribution, no matter the size, helps. Thank you."

   What It Means: By reminding visitors that it relies exclusively on grassroots support and operates on a shoestring budget, ColorOfChange.org sends the message that donations will go further with this organization than they might with a larger, more lobbyist- and corporation-friendly organization, where your hard-earned money might just be another drop in the bucket.

Figure 6.2
Volunteers for the Tzu Chi Foundation raise funds on the streets of Chicago, to benefit survivors of a Mississippi River flood. Photo: © 2008 Vera Yu and David Li. Licensed under Creative Commons Attribution License 2.0 Generic.

- **MoveOn.org**

  https://pol.moveon.org/donate/donate.html

  What It Says: "Through MoveOn.org Political Action, you can change who has influence in politics—from a few big-money donors to a massive number of small donors. It's a way to reward candidates who take a stand for us, support challengers driven by progressive values, and demonstrate grassroots support for those willing to fight for our interests."

  What It Means: Like ColorOfChange.org, MoveOn.org emphasizes the grassroots nature of the organization and the non-grassroots nature of other organizations competing for funds. But because MoveOn.org focuses on winning elections rather than the more issue-oriented civil rights campaigns of ColorOfChange, its language is less hopeful and more pragmatic—almost Machiavellian.

- **Parents, Friends, and Families of Lesbians and Gays (PFLAG)**

  http://community.pflag.org/Page.aspx?pid=459

  What It Says: "As a supporter of PFLAG, you enable us to expand our work to keep families together, educate the public and advocate for equal rights and fair treatment for GLBT people and their families. ***Click here*** to learn more about the programs and services your contributions make possible."

  What It Means: PFLAG doesn't turn down corporate contributions, and its older, more moderate donor base is unlikely to be impressed by the David-and-Goliath grassroots rhetoric of more politically focused organizations—but one common denominator that appeals to all donors is a page explaining where the money goes.

- **National Council of La Raza (NCLR)**

  https://secure.groundspring.org/dn/index.php?id=1955

  What It Says: "By joining NCLR you are saying that you want to make an impact on the lives of Hispanic Americans. NCLR strives to reshape the future that lies ahead for the Hispanic community by improving access to education, health care, financial independence, and homeownership. Why not help make that impact?"

  What It Means: Like PFLAG (but with a much, much larger budget), NCLR relies on a mix of grassroots, big-donor, and corporate support to do its considerable work. It needs a message that appeals to a broad range of demographics, and it finds one in three simple sentences: (1) your donation sends a message that you care about Latinos in the United States, (2) your donation will constructively improve the quality of life for Latino communities (among others), and (3) there's no good reason not to be part of this effort. Very compact and, from the looks of things, very effective.

- **Southern Poverty Law Center**

  https://secure.splcenter.org/donate/online/online.jsp

  What It Says: "Your gift will help win justice on behalf of those who have no other champion, expose and fight the hate that thrives in our country, and provide tolerance education materials free of charge to schools across our nation."

  What It Means: Exactly what it says. The SPLC's donation statement is among the simplest and most straightforward you'll find—it just tells you three efforts your money will directly support. The goal here, as always, is to explain why you are not wasting the money you donate.

Finding Grants Online

Donations aren't the only potential source of income for your organization; if your organization addresses a community need, it could be eligible for grant funding. Among the more useful sites for searches

- Grants.gov (www.grants.gov)—The U.S. government gives out billions of dollars in grants every year, and you can search for appropriate grants—at no charge!—through its official grants database site.

- The Foundation Center (www.fdncenter.org)—The Foundation Center's database isn't free (the basic plan is $20 per month), but it's one of the larger private nonprofit grant databases.

> > > N O T E

For more about grants (and how to apply for them), check out *Non-Profit Guides: Grant-Writing Tools for Non-Profit Organizations* at http://www.npguides.org/.

So considering the preceding examples, I'd say there's a good five-step process you can follow with respect to how you go about asking for money:

1. **Figure out where it's going**—Be dramatic, but honest. (Figure 6.3, released by UNICEF, is a good illustration of this principle.)

2. **Figure out where it's been**—Does your organization have a plucky David-and-Goliath story to tell? Does it have a history of relying on grassroots support? Does it rely primarily on small donations? Does it reject corporate donations? Is the donation tax deductible?

3. **Figure out what it means**—If donating to your organization is a great way to show that you care about puppies, or oppose [insert evil political movement here], then you may as well say so.

4. **Decide which part of this story to emphasize**—You might choose to emphasize all the preceding steps, but more than likely a narrative will come out of the picture. Remember to keep your pitch simple—all the previous examples run from one to three sentences, and that's all that most site visitors unfamiliar with your organization are likely to read.

5. **Keep the connections visible**—Whenever possible, make sure a donation link is always easily accessible on your organization's website and as a link in any email newsletters or action alerts.

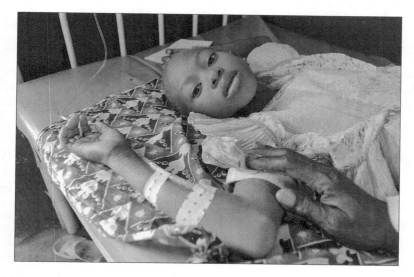

Figure 6.3

A young patient receives health care services at the Sam Ouandja refugee camp in the Central African Republic, a potentially lifesaving intervention made possible by UNICEF funding. Photo: © 2008 Pierre Holtz / UNICEF. Licensed under Creative Commons Attribution License 2.0 Generic.

Other Ways to Raise Funds

Asking for donations outright isn't necessarily the only way to raise money from online supporters. Here are a few that have been tried:

- **Online Memberships**—Most nonprofit organizations offer memberships. If yours doesn't yet, consider creating a members-only section of your website and charging a nominal annual fee for access to it.

What Can I Offer Members?

If your organization is small, or even if it isn't, you might be asking yourself what you'd put on a members-only website to make it worth your time and their money. Here are seven ideas:

- Discounts or free tickets to your organization's events.

- Online activist training.

- Access to conference calls.

- Discounts on any materials your organization might ordinarily sell (branded logo items, for example).

- A private, members-only mailing list or online discussion forum.

- A private, members-only email newsletter.

- Printable membership cards and other printable materials.

If all of this sounds like more work, that's because it is—and it might be worth the time and effort. If you think members will want to join just to support your organization's work and wouldn't know what to do with a members-only site if you did set one up, then there are probably more constructive ways to spend your time, energy, and resources.

- **Educational Programs**—Distance learning is hot (just look at Appendix E), and there's no reason in principle why you couldn't, or shouldn't, offer an online class for a fee and grant a certificate upon completion. Just make sure you don't grant a *degree*, as this can be problematic for many reasons (state licensure requirements, accreditation issues, résumé scandals—you don't want to go there).

- **T-Shirts and Other Merchandise**—Selling T-shirts is a time-honored way to raise money for organizations, and using CafePress (http://www.cafepress.com) you can choose to print your organization's logo or another message on anything from T-shirts to wall clocks to messenger bags to thongs. CafePress handles payment, production, and distribution itself, so there's no need for you to worry about processing orders; you just design the materials, pay a nominal monthly fee, and your organization can collect the checks from there.

On the Books...

There are 28 different kinds of 501(c) organizations, from 501(c)(1)s (which include most corporations founded by Congress) to 501(c)(28)s (a railroad retirement Trust established by the government in 2001). The two most common types of 501(c) organizations are 501(c)(3)s, which include most charitable and educational organizations, and 501(c)(4)s, which include most lobbying groups. Donations to 501(c)(3) organizations are tax-deductible; donations to 501(c)(4) organizations are not.

I'm assuming that if you're soliciting donations as an organization, you've registered as a 501(c) nonprofit of some kind. If you haven't, check out the USA.gov on registering a nonprofit organization (it's not all that hard, although it does sometimes involve a fee):

http://www.usa.gov/Business/Nonprofit_State.shtml

Some organizations solicit donations without actually registering as nonprofits, but I don't recommend it. There's no significant oversight, and potential donors know it.

Processing Online Donations

Okay, so now you know *how* to solicit donations. But if a supporter says yes, where do you go from there?

No matter how you accept funds, unless you're given cash donations, there is always an intermediary. Even if someone mails you a check, it has to be deposited at a bank. This is good for record-keeping, but it can be inconvenient if you don't have a way to get from point A to point B.

- **Accepting Checks and Money Orders**—Not everybody is comfortable giving out credit card information online, so whenever possible, include an address on your donation page where donations by check or money order may be sent.

- **Accepting Credit Cards Directly**—All the organizations discussed earlier in this chapter accept credit cards directly because they've budgeted for it, but this can get expensive and complicated because you'll need both a secure server and a credit card processing service of some kind (usually a merchant account works out best, but alternatives exist). All this requires substantial investment of both time and money up front. If you're just starting out with online donations, you're better off using an intermediary service; it doesn't become cost-effective to do otherwise until you're receiving a *lot* of online donations.

- **Accepting Payments by SMS Text**—Following the January 2010 Haiti earthquake, the American Red Cross successfully raised over $24 million for survivors by using MGive (http://www.mgive.com), a service that allows donors to contribute money to an organization simply by texting a message to a cell phone number (the donation is automatically charged to the sender's cell phone bill). While MGive is expensive—costs include a 3.5% per-transaction fee and a monthly service charge of $399 to $1,499—this is a growing high-tech option for large organizations and may become affordable for smaller organizations as well.

- **Accepting Credit Cards Through PayPal**—The most commonly used intermediary service is PayPal, which offers a special rate to nonprofit organizations seeking donations (www.paypal.com/nonprofit). At present, the rate for a 501(c)(3) nonprofit is 1.9% plus 30 cents per transaction for volume up to $100,000 per month (the rate increases to 2.2% plus 30 cents per transaction if you receive more than $100,000 per month in donations; this is a much better deal than the 2.9% transaction rate PayPal offers small for-profit organizations). If someone donates $50 through PayPal, for example, your organization will take in $48.75 of the money, after PayPal deducts $1.25 in processing fees (95 cents being 1.9% of $50, plus the 30-cent per-donation charge). If someone donates $200,000 through PayPal, PayPal deducts $4,400.30 (2.2% of $200,000 plus 30 cents) and your organization gets $195,599.70. And because the entire process is administered by PayPal, your organization never actually gets the credit card information, so encrypting it and keeping it secure is less of a concern.

- **Accepting Credit Cards Through Other Intermediary Services**—Other organizations process online donations for nonprofits—three that are often talked about are NetworkForGood (www.networkforgood.org), JustGive (www.justgive.org), and CharityAdvantage (www.charityadvantage.org)—but for most small nonprofits soliciting donations online, these are less cost-effective inasmuch as they deduct higher rates (2.9% to 3% per transaction instead of the 1.9% to 2.2% required by PayPal), and NetworkForGood and CharityAdvantage also charge monthly fees. Still, it's worth investigating these options because of the additional services they provide to nonprofits, such as automatic tax receipts for donors and optional web hosting.

Could Kiva.org Save the World?

If you're looking for heroes who could solve the problem of global poverty, you could do worse than Muhammad Yunus, 2006 Nobel Peace Prize recipient and director of Bangladesh's Grameen Bank (www.grameen-info.org), which has given out more than US $6B in small loans under favorable terms to 7 million low-income individuals who would not have been eligible for traditional loans. These individuals have used the loans as seed money to create businesses that now form the backbone of Grameen, which has a repayment rate of 98%, has actually turned over a profit, and has operated on its own, without donations, since 1995.

The principle behind Grameen is simple: Small amounts of discretionary income from the world's wealthy can provide seed money for sustainable economies among the world's poor—in the process destroying predatory lending practices that have crippled the development of regional economies. In his 2006 Nobel Lecture, Yunus explained how he developed the concept of microlending:

> I was shocked to discover a woman in the village, borrowing less than a dollar from the money-lender, on the condition that he would have the exclusive right to buy all she produces at the price he decides. This, to me, was a way of recruiting slave labor.

> I decided to make a list of the victims of this money-lending 'business' in the village next door to our campus.

> When my list was done, it had the names of 42 victims who borrowed a total amount of US $27. I offered US $27 from my own pocket to get these victims out of the clutches of those money-lenders. The excitement that was created among the people by this small action got me further involved in it. If I could make so many people so happy with such a tiny amount of money, why not do more of it?

But setting up as a Grameen investor can be tricky. In 2003, global poverty activists Matt Flannery and Jessica Jackley heard Yunus speak at Stanford Business School and began to get involved in microlending. Deciding that the Internet was a perfect venue for this sort of thing—as it would connect wealthy donors in industrialized nations to entrepreneurs in the poorest areas of the world, maximizing the benefit of microlending—they cofounded Kiva (Swahili: "unity") in 2005. According to its website, it has since distributed $95.3 million in loans to 135,782 entrepreneurs in 49 countries, with a 98.42% repayment rate. The effect on developing economies is immeasurable.

Your E-Activism Toolkit: Raising Money

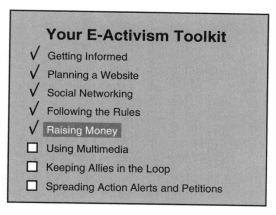

Confession: I do my activism in Jackson, Mississippi, capital of the nation's poorest state. There's not much money to play with, so I've learned from the best when it comes to working on a shoestring budget. The vast majority of online activism options in this book don't cost anything at all, and for the rest I've tried to keep things as cheap as possible.

So really, I don't want to overemphasize this chapter, but I do want to point out ways that the money you raise here could help elsewhere.

- **Getting Informed**—A few of the research websites, most notably Questia, cost money; money can also buy courtesy card access at your local university library or cover magazine subscriptions.

- **Building a Website**—Domain hosting costs money (usually less than $100/year), but if you really want to hire a web designer, you can shell out $500 to $1,000 to some local guru and get something fancier than a non-expert volunteer could probably design.

- **Using Multimedia**—You can license out content, buy more expensive photography and videorecording equipment, and upgrade your Flickr account.

- **Keeping Allies in the Loop**—You can pay for a commercial newsletter service (and cover any SMS charges).

For that matter, if you've got enough money and aren't inclined to do any of this online activism stuff yourself, I suppose you can put this book down and hire out a specialist, in which case I suppose this is goodbye.

But if you're still here, let's talk about multimedia in the next chapter. And I'll keep it cheap, I promise.

How to Use Multimedia as an Activism Tool

"I longed for a power of vision which might overpass that limit; which might reach the busy world, towns, regions full of life I had heard of but never seen…I could not help it: the restlessness was in my nature; it agitated me to pain sometimes."

—Charlotte Brontë, *Jane Eyre* (1847)

The oldest recorded forms of human communication are not words, but rather paintings and sculptures. About 30,000 years ago, an anonymous group of ancient humans wandered into the Chauvet-Pont-d'Arc Cave in southern France and left a beautiful mess, drawing hyenas and other wild animals, making handprints on the wall, and generally leaving an impression. A few thousand years later, another group wandered in and added more art. The collection grew, a sort of ancient gallery, and was then forgotten, most likely neglected for tens of thousands of years, until its rediscovery in 1994.

Words are central to our identity as a species, but there is something iconic, something sacred, about a shared image. These ancient paintings don't just communicate facts about the creatures that our ancient human ancestors saw; they communicate how those creatures looked to our ancient human ancestors. As we look at the eyes, fur, and necks of these long-dead animals (see Figure 7.1), as we contemplate the long-dead calloused fingers that reproduced them on the cold, stone cave walls, we have the opportunity to look at the world through their eyes.

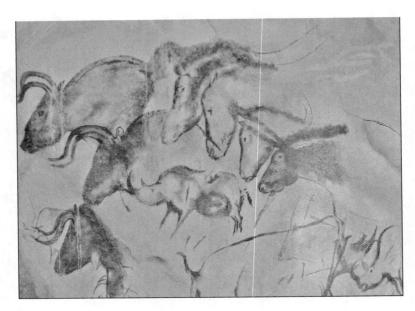

Figure 7.1
Detail from ancient paintings found in the Chauvet Pont-d' Arc Cave in southeastern France. Photo: Released into the public domain by the photographer, Wikipedia contributor HTO.

Direct communication—of pictures, moving images, and sound—can serve many functions in activism. It can serve as record, as evidence, as illustration, or as art. Sometimes it serves all of these functions at once. Early on, the Internet was primarily about words. But we're rediscovering the power of images and sounds, and this gives us new, effective tools as activists.

Online Multimedia Content That Changed the World

In an activism context, it's tempting to look at multimedia as decoration or advertising. It serves those purposes well; a PowerPoint presentation (see Figure 7.2) is much easier on the eyes than a chalkboard, even though it serves essentially the same purpose. Multimedia is pretty, and if that's all it was, it would still be worth using.

But there's more to multimedia than that. As these examples show, online multimedia is already an effective instrument of activism.

Figure 7.2
A student learns how to use PowerPoint as part of Dublin City University's Irish-language business and information technology degree program. Photo: © 2009 Fiontar at Dublin City University. Licensed under Creative Commons Attribution License 2.0 Generic.

The Iranian Protests of 2009

When Mahmoud Ahmadinejad claimed victory over Mir Hossein Mousavi in the 2009 Iranian elections, the people of Iran weren't buying it. Activists took to the streets in record numbers, taking pictures and recording video of massive crowds that according to the government did not exist, taking pictures and recording videos of police brutality and deaths that according to the government did not occur. The international media caught wind of all this, and the Iranian human rights movement received so much visible support that even conservative legislative leaders in the Iranian government expressed concern that the election results might have been forged. While the Ayatollah Khamenei has reaffirmed the outcome following an alleged official investigation, the government of Iran has been shaken to its core—with images of crowds and popular uprising not seen since the Shah was overthrown in 1979.

The historical parallels between the multimedia generated by the protests and memories of the 1979 Revolution were not lost on Iranian pro-democracy activists, who have successfully used both iconic, empowering images of courageous protest (see Figure 7.3) and distressing, scandalous images of government misconduct to provide the visual vocabulary of their movement. The Internet has made these images available to everyone—in a manner that leaves no paper trail.

Figure 7.3
Pro-democracy demonstrators take to the streets of Tehran to call for government oversight of election returns. Photo: © 2009 Hamed Saber. Licensed under Creative Commons Attribution License 2.0 Generic.

The Burmese Protests of 2007

From August to November 2007, thousands of monks, nuns, and ordinary citizens marched against the Burmese military dictatorship. When the government was unable to quash the protests by usual police means, it took more direct violent action—assaulting thousands and killing hundreds. Photographs and video of the junta's military police battering monks and nuns have shocked the world and drawn attention to the military regime, forcing it to begin negotiations with opposition leaders. Although early indications suggest that these negotiations are nothing more than a stalling tactic, the fact that the leadership feels a stalling tactic to be necessary indicates the strength of the protests.

The Burmese pro-democracy movement has long been able to use iconic portraits of Aung San Suu Kyi, the legitimate victor of Burma's 1990 national elections (who has been subjected to house arrest in the 20 years since). But the multimedia generated by the 2007 protests also draws a clear distinction between the country's national religious establishment (see Figure 7.4) and the oppressive government. The government has been branded out as a violent force that is not only opposed to the will of the people, but also to religious tradition. This is good PR for pro-democracy activism in Burma—and lethal PR for its government.

Figure 7.4

Thousands of monks and other pro-democracy demonstrators protest the oppressive Myanmar regime in Burma. Photo: © 2007 racoles (via Flickr). Licensed under Creative Commons Attribution License 2.0 Generic.

Abu Ghraib

Rumors of torture in U.S. detention facilities following the attacks of September 11, 2001, were rampant in the early years of the Bush administration's War on Terror, but proof of the abuses was notoriously hard to come by. Then *60 Minutes II* broadcast leaked images (such as Figure 7.5) depicting the sexual assault, abuse, and murders of prisoners at the U.S.-operated Abu Ghraib Prison in Baghdad, Iraq. The images were redistributed on the Internet (where they reached a much larger audience), and Abu Ghraib became an international scandal.

Human rights groups, such as the American Civil Liberties Union (ACLU) and Amnesty International, made good use of these images online to show why regulation of U.S. interrogation protocol was needed. The Obama administration officially banned torture by executive order in January 2009; while it is not entirely clear that this ban is adequate, it very likely would not have been proposed at all were it not for the efforts of activists to distribute these incriminating photos.

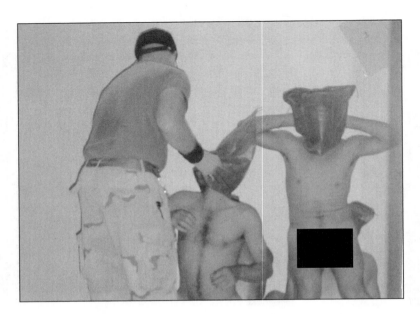

Figure 7.5
U.S. personnel torture detainees at Abu Ghraib Prison in Baghdad, Iraq. Public domain. Photo: U.S. Department of Defense.

Justice for Oscar Grant

On New Year's Eve, 2008, a group of police officers patrolling Bay Area Rapid Transit (BART) in Oakland, California, detained a group of young black men based on reports of a fight on a subway car. Officers singled out 22-year-old grocery store butcher Oscar Grant, who witnesses said was not involved in the altercation, and ordered him to lie facedown on the concrete. After he did so, Officer Joe Mehserle pulled out a revolver and shot him to death. The shooting, which could have been dismissed as "self-defense" if there had not been any witnesses deemed credible by investigators, was captured on multiple cell phone cameras and distributed both over the Internet and through local news media. As a result, Mehserle has been arrested and charged with murder.

The video of the shooting itself made Mehserle's arrest possible, but multimedia documenting the reaction of African-American groups all over the country (see Figure 7.6) has placed additional pressure on law enforcement agencies in California to take the shooting seriously. The shooting has also contributed to the growth of Copwatch law enforcement surveillance programs, in which citizens are encouraged to monitor and document the behavior of police.

Figure 7.6
Demonstrators carry a mock casket representing the body of Oscar Grant, shot to death by Bay Area Rapid Transit police on New Year's Day 2009. Photo: © 2009 Jacob Ruff. Licensed under Creative Commons Attribution License 2.0 Generic.

"Macaque"

Nobody would have accused former governor and U.S. Senator George Allen (R-VA) of being particularly sensitive on race issues; a noose had hung in his law office before he entered politics, and he had a great love for the Confederacy, declaring April to be Confederate History and Heritage Month during his tenure as governor (officially praising the South's role in the American Civil War as "a four-year struggle for independence and sovereign rights"). But when video surfaced on YouTube of Allen using a racial epithet against an opponent's staffer, it ended his career as a national politician.

It was easy for Allen to spot S.R. Sidarth, a local college student, as a supporter of his opponent—Sidarth was the only nonwhite person in the crowd at an August 2006 rally, and his Indian-American ancestry was obvious. When he pointed to Sidarth and said "Let's give a welcome to macaque here. Welcome to America and the real world of Virginia," he used as a racial epithet popular among white French Tunisians (Allen's mother being a white French Tunisian)—by referring to a dark-skinned person as a "macaque," a species of monkey—he attracted the wrong kind of public attention. He lost the election to Democrat Jim Webb and has not been taken seriously as a political candidate since.

The 2006 May Day Protests in MacArthur Park

The Day Without Immigrants protests of May 1st, 2007, a series of marches held at major cities all over the country (see Figure 7.7) in an effort to protect the civil rights of undocumented workers, largely went off without a hitch. But in MacArthur Park in Los Angeles, after protestors were late in leaving the park, the police lost control, attacking both protestors and journalists covering the rally—even attacking television cameras, presumably in an attempt to destroy evidence. Cell phone cameras captured the incident on video; after the video went viral, thousands marched in protest against the LAPD's actions. Nineteen officers are still under investigation for their role in the beatings.

Figure 7.7
Detail from the Day Without Latinos immigration reform march in Milwaukee, Wisconsin, in May 2007. Photo: © 2007 Voces de la Frontera. Licensed under Creative Commons Attribution License 2.0 Generic.

Online Video and How to Stream It

So let's say you've got streaming video of your own, or belonging to your organization, that you're authorized to upload and plan to upload. What next?

All the following options are free:

- **YouTube**—www.youtube.com

    YouTube is the most popular online video hosting service, and unless you have a personal preference for one of the others, it's the only one you'll really need to deal with.

On YouTube you can upload streaming video, set up a channel for videos related to your topic, and network with other users in a video-focused social network. YouTube even offers code that you can cut-and-paste into your website so people can view your YouTube videos on your own site without having to visit youtube.com. Of course, the services that follow offer the same options.

- **Dailymotion**—www.dailymotion.com

The main advantage of French-run Dailymotion is that it supports HTML 5, which allows browsers to display videos inline without using an Adobe Flash player. In the long run, this is a good thing because it means less reliance on proprietary web standards. In the short run, it's mostly a symbolic gesture; Flash and HTML 5 work in roughly the same way, and only the newest browsers can accommodate the latter.

- **LiveVideo**—www.livevideo.com

As the name suggests, the main advantage of LiveVideo is that it allows you to go live rather than uploading already saved videos.

If you've put videos online with YouTube or another service, make sure you provide a link to your organization's or cause's YouTube page on your website, social networking fan page, and so forth so that users can visit.

Online Streaming Video

What You'll Need:

A digital video recorder, which can range in price from $90 on up, and video editing software, which can be free (see www.versiontracker.com) or range in the hundreds of dollars

How It Works:

1. Record video on your digital video recorder.

2. Download it to your machine from the video recorder.

3. Make any necessary changes using video editing software.

4. Upload it to one of the video sharing sites described here.

> > > NOTE

Note also that some social networks, including both MySpace and Facebook (see Chapter 4), let users host videos that can be viewed by other members of the social network without relying on a third-party service like YouTube, although YouTube videos can also be viewed on the sites.

Online Photography

What You'll Need:

A digital camera, which comes with many cell phones or can be purchased at low cost, and photo editing software, which can be free (see www.versiontracker.com) or range in the hundreds of dollars

How It Works:

1. Take photographs on your digital camera.

2. Download them to your machine from the camera.

3. Make any necessary changes using photo editing software.

4. Upload it to Flickr and/or to the social networking sites described in Chapter 4.

- **My Friend Flickr**—If you've taken photos of events and would like to host them, in much the same way you might host online videos, Flickr (www.flickr.com) is probably what you need. Why use Flickr instead of just sticking the photos up on your organization's social networking page? Well, it doesn't hurt to do both, but Flickr offers some advantages of its own:

  - Photos can be made available to everyone, not just members of the relevant social network.

  - Photos can be linked to other, similarly themed pictures by linking them to tags or groups. For example:

    www.flickr.com/photos/tags/activism/

    www.flickr.com/groups/socialchange/

  - Flickr hosts higher-resolution photographs than most social networks can—up to 1024 pixels in dimension for free users and any photo up to 20MB for paid Pro users.

  - Flickr has more flexible terms of service regarding the content of photographs (allowing, for example, breastfeeding photos).

  - Free users can display up to 200 photos on Flickr at a time; Pro users can display a virtually unlimited number of photos. Flickr Pro access costs $25 per year.

Finding Photographs You Can Use

There are plenty of resources you can use to put multimedia out there, but what if you *need* photos for your web or print materials?

Here are the resources I use to locate public domain and "copylefted" (copyrighted but free-to-use) images:

- **Wikimedia Commons**—http://commons.wikimedia.org

  With 5 million files, Wikimedia Commons is the first place to look for any and all public domain and copylefted materials. Be sure to check the specific license of the photo you're looking for (which will be provided on the page); some photographs must be attributed to their source; others can't be modified or adapted; and still others have different, specific restrictions. But almost everything in this database can be put to use for your cause at no charge.

- **Flickr/Creative Commons**—www.flickr.com/creativecommons

  Flickr has a special database of 125 million (yes, 125 million) photos that have been uploaded with Creative Commons licenses and can be reused. They tend to be personal photographs, but many of them are quite good.

- **The Library of Congress: Prints and Photographs Catalog**— http://lcweb2.loc.gov/pp/pphome.html

  Most of the 1.2 million images in this searchable online collection are in the public domain, but be sure to check copyright status on the image's main page just to be sure. Although the database is heavily slanted toward photographs of historical importance ("theodore roosevelt" returns 661 matches, "einstein" 88, "gandhi" 56), plenty of other material—from posters to old cartoons to Ansel Adams' photographs of Japanese-American internment camps—can be found here. Unless your topic is very new, this may be the best place to look first.

- **The Archival Research Catalog (ARC) of the National Archives**— www.archives.gov/research/arc/

  Although NARA-ARC is much smaller than the Library of Congress's online prints and photographs catalog, hosting only 153,000 digital images, it's still a great place to look for public domain photos. NARA's pictures tend to be lower-resolution than the Library of Congress's, but they're more often in color.

The Art of Podcasting

A podcast is an Internet television or radio program. It is no different in practice from a traditional television or radio program; the only difference is the medium.

There isn't really much to podcasting. If you're doing a video podcast, just create a YouTube account for it and upload the new episodes as you finish them. If you're doing an audio podcast, record an MP3 regularly, upload it to your website, and make it visible and accessible every time you release a new episode.

The trouble is getting people to *watch* or *hear* it. I recommend putting links to new podcast entries on a blog (more on blogs in the next chapter), posting a new blog linking to each new piece every time a new edition comes out. If you want a large audience, it's also a good idea to submit your podcast to iTunes (www.apple.com/itunes/podcasts/specs.html).

The only practical drawback to podcasts is that not many people have figured out how to make money off them yet. If you're working or volunteering for an organization, or just want to promote a cause, this probably isn't going to be a huge issue for you.

Online Audio

What You'll Need:

An ordinary microphone that plugs into your computer (which can be purchased for as little as $5) or a built-in computer microphone, and audio recording or editing software, which can be free (see www.versiontracker.com) or range in the hundreds of dollars

How It Works:

1. Record audio on your microphone using audio recording/editing software.

2. Make any necessary changes.

3. Upload it to your website (see Chapter 3) and/or a free podcast-hosting site such as PodBean (www.podbean.com).

Great Podcasts for Activists

Just as the key to good writing is to read, the key to good podcasting is to watch and listen. These podcasts provide information that may be useful to you as an activist and may also give you a sense of what works and what doesn't.

*   **Idealist.org Podcast**—www.idealist.org/en/podcast/index.html

    This podcast is all about activism—featuring interviews with real activists and information on strategies that your cause/organization can put to use.

*   **52 Ways to Change the World! with Julie Zauzmer**—http://julie.libsyn.com/

    Each week's podcast features a "fun, quick, and easy way to bring charity into your daily life."

*   **Five Good Things in the World (MHz Networks)**—www.mhznetworks.org/broadband/

    A weekly video podcast showing five positive developments in the world. Uplifting but also practical because it not only provides positive news, but usually gives some indication of how things got so darned positive in the first place.

*   **Bioneers**—www.bioneers.org/radio/bioneers-podcast/

    Bioneers profiles and interviews people who are changing the world, from *Vagina Monologues* author and anti-violence campaigner Eve Ensler to ColorOfChange.org cofounder Van Jones.

- **Democracy Now! with Amy Goodman**—www.democracynow.org

  Democracy Now! (available in both video and audio formats) is the daily voice of the international antiwar Left and occasionally features in-depth interviews and ground-breaking investigative reporting.

- **Cato Weekly Video**—www.cato.org/weekly/

  The weekly video podcast of the right-wing libertarian Cato Institute is thoughtful, well-produced, and cogent. Watching both this and Democracy Now! on a regular basis may make you too much of an independent thinker to function comfortably in a political campaign, but it'll improve your ability to write good talking points.

- **Bill Moyers: Journal (PBS)**—www.pbs.org/moyers/journal/index-flash.html

  This weekly interview series by longtime journalist and documentarian Bill Moyers looks at social issues from a nuanced and thoughtful perspective. Centering on interviews, onsite reports, and raw data, Moyers asks difficult questions of his audience and guests. Video and audio.

- **Washington Week with Gwen Ifill (PBS)**—www.pbs.org/weta/washingtonweek/video/

  Longtime interviewer Gwen Ifill talks to real journalists about politics, rather than the usual talking heads that appear on these kinds of programs, and the results are much more useful from a policy analysis point of view.

- **Amanpour: The Power of the Interview (CNN)**— www.cnn.com/CNNI/Programs/amanpour/

  Christiane Amanpour is arguably the best international investigative journalist you'll find, and her daily world report program functions as a U.S. counterpart to the BBC World News. If your activism involves global issues in any way, you would probably be well-served to at least watch the Friday edition, which summarizes the top stories of the week. Audio and video are both available.

- **Fareed Zakaria: GPS (CNN)**—www.cnn.com/CNN/Programs/fareed.zakaria.gps/

  Zakaria (author of the bestselling *The Future of Freedom*) is more of a theoretician than Amanpour, so his show focuses more on panels and policy questions and less on interviews and investigative reporting—which is not a bad thing, just a different thing. If you do activism on any international issues, you might be well-served to try them both.

- **Washington Post/Washington Post HD**—www.washingtonpost.com/wp-srv/mme-dia/podcastfront.htm

  The title series focuses on a specific in-the-news topic every week, providing video to review and supplement the paper's coverage. Other Washington Post podcasts, such as P3: Post Politics Podcast and onBeing, have a more thematic approach. Podcasts are available in audio, video, and HD.

- **bloggingheads.tv**—www.bloggingheads.tv

  You won't find many video podcasts that are more web savvy than this one, and the cheeky sense of humor—and in-depth approach—it uses with the activists, scholars, bloggers, and other thinkers it interviews make it a must-watch.

- **Big Vision with Britt Bravo**—http://bigvisionpodcast.libsyn.com/

  Bravo, a consultant focusing on nonprofit strategies, offers up interviews with activists and other nonprofit leaders who have accomplished things and asks them how they pulled it off.

- **Social Good with Allison Fine**—http://philanthropy.com/media/audio/socialgood/

  This monthly podcast from the author of *Momentum: Igniting Social Change in the Connected Age* is sponsored by the *Chronicle of Philanthropy* and focuses on charity and nonprofits.

- **Forum with Michael Krasny (KQED)**—www.kqed.org/radio/programs/forum/

  Forum has an unmistakable Northern California focus, but Krasny has an unmistakable gift for interviewing and policy analysis.

- **Mother Jones Podcast**—www.motherjones.com/rss/podcast

  This podcast sometimes follows the investigative-reporting focus of the magazine, sometimes rounds up stories the magazine has already told, and sometimes is just made up of interviews with interesting people. It's Mother Jones; if you're familiar with the magazine you already have a pretty good idea of what you're getting into, and if you don't, and you're an activist of any description, you should check it out.

- **Tell Me More (NPR)**—www.npr.org/templates/rundowns/rundown.php?prgId=46

  Hosted by Michel Martin, Tell Me More "focuses on the way we live, intersect and collide in a culturally diverse world." Panels and interviews centering on race, culture, class, and gender intersect to create an interesting show that is as much about culture as it is about policy.

- **My History Can Beat Up Your Politics**—
  http://myhistorycanbeatupyourpolitics.blogspot.com

  Bruce Carlson's podcast applies the context of history to the policy debates of today, giving a good indication (at times) of how things got the way they are, how they have changed, and how they haven't. It's a good antidote to the apocalyptic tone that social justice activism can sometimes have.

- **Documentaries (BBC)**—www.bbc.co.uk/podcasts/series/docarchive/

  The BBC's short radio documentaries are fascinating, covering a topic in detail in less than 30 minutes. The British accent comes standard at no charge.

- **Think with Krys Boyd (KERA)**—www.kera.org/think/

Boyd asks questions about policy and current events that just don't come up during mainstream discussions of a topic. Everybody knows that Bernie Madoff perpetrated the largest Wall Street investment fraud incident in history; Krys Boyd sits down with the author of a Madoff biography and spends an hour asking *why* he did it.

Your E-Activism Toolkit: Using Multimedia

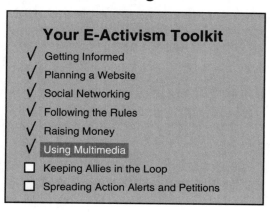

Two things to keep in mind about multimedia:

- Nobody has ever gotten in trouble just for making *excessive* use of high-quality multimedia or being *too* savvy about image and entertaining potential supporters. This is not something you're likely to overdo. On the other hand...

- Multimedia is a tool, so it can't provide sustenance for your movement all on its own.

The question to ask yourself about multimedia technology is the same question to ask yourself about all other technology that can potentially be adapted for an activism purpose: What am I trying to *accomplish* with this?

If there's a talking point you're trying to put out there that you think you can illustrate better using multimedia, have at it. If you're using multimedia just to read off existing talking points in a way that isn't any more interesting than letting the reader take a gander at them in print, then that probably isn't an effective use of the medium.

Online activism is a means to an end. It is not an end unto itself. There is nothing special or mystical about multimedia that will spoil an otherwise good effort or save an otherwise bad one. It's just another language, another way to speak to people. Some might be more receptive to it than they would be to more traditional media, but the important part is still the message, the story it tells.

How to Keep Allies and Supporters in the Loop

"It does not matter what you know about anything if you cannot communicate to your people. In that event, you are not even a failure. You're just not there."

—Saul Alinsky

Here's something you're not going to see on the front page of your local daily: "Environmental group sends newsletter, announces monthly meeting." Most of what *looks* like activism is really about attracting interest and bringing people in (see Figure 8.1), not the cause itself. Being attention grabbing is fun, exciting, and glamorous. Paying attention to something for a long period of time is—well, more like work. But it's the most important part. The sizzle sells the steak, but the sizzle isn't very filling.

It's like with relationships. Want to meet the love of your life? There are authors and motivational speakers who would be happy to sell you books, hundreds and hundreds of books, explaining how they say you can do that. But after the honeymoon's over (and that cliché exists for a reason), keeping a relationship together takes real work on both sides. It makes you wonder how many people who say they're looking for the love of their lives really mean it, and how many of us are like dogs chasing ice cream trucks—fascinated with the journey, not quite sure what we'd do if we ever reached the destination.

Figure 8.1
Members of United Steelworkers (USW Local 2-232, Milwaukee) share flyers publicizing an upcoming event. Photo: © 2008 Bernard Pollack. Licensed under Creative Commons Attribution License 2.0 Generic.

I believe that the best way to figure out what will keep someone in a movement is to figure out what got them there in the first place. If you attracted hundreds of people to sweat and yell and wave picket signs, finding reasons to do that on a regular basis—there are good ones—may help keep their interest. That isn't to say that this is *all* you should do (there's something to be said for variety), but be conscious of the activities and online content that seems to engage people most. And respect the fact that no matter how committed someone is to an ideology, he won't be able to get enthusiastic about doing things that he finds to be drudgery or an unproductive waste of time. He has to be spiritually fed.

Online media makes it hard to do that because it's so perfect for advertising that organizations advertise for members and then advertise for membership renewals. They advertise for first-time donors and then advertise again to get more donations. And this works, up to a point, especially if we're advertising a movement that people want to see succeed. But we need to never lose sight of the fact that the movement is made up of people whose attention we've *already* gotten, and we need to devise ways to help keep them involved.

In the Roman Catholic and Anglican traditions, someone who has joined, who has formally been confirmed as a member, is called a communicant in good standing. That sounds good, doesn't it? The word "communicant" comes from *communion* rather than *communication*, but we can introduce an ambiguous folk etymology and say that we're all, no matter what our cause, looking for our own communicants in good standing. We're looking for people to join us at the table, people to break bread with as we go forward week by week and try to change the world.

Silence Is Not Golden

Activist volunteers and donors usually do what they do not because you or your organization have persuaded them that they need to make the world better, but rather because they've always wanted to make the world better and you or your organization have provided them with a possible vehicle for doing that. If they can't accomplish their goals within your group, they'll usually move on—sometimes to another cause—and find other opportunities to satisfy their altruistic impulses.

So if someone is interested and engaged enough to write you an email, it makes sense to reply to it.

Yes, some extremely talkative souls will send you a landfill's worth of messages, and you're entitled to write off the cranks. But with few exceptions, it is *always* a good idea to reply to emails—even if your reply is late. This is more for psychological than practical reasons: the person shows interest and nothing happens, and he or she may feel ignored or powerless within the organization.

If you want people to stay interested, members and supporters need to feel like there's a *point* to being interested. If their attempts to contact the organization don't go anywhere, they probably won't keep trying.

Not Necessarily the Newsletter

You don't necessarily need to do a regular weekly, biweekly, or monthly e-newsletter to keep interest going in your movement; regular announcements will work. (Action alerts, described in the next chapter, are especially helpful.) And if you do a newsletter, it doesn't necessarily need to be fancy. The important thing is to tell subscribers what needs to be said—whatever that happens to be for your organization or cause. Whatever you do, I personally recommend starting with no more than a small newsletter, published regularly and as infrequently as you're willing to tolerate. That way you don't start off with a larger or more frequently published newsletter and then reduce its size and/or frequency, which leaves subscribers with the feeling that there's not as much interesting stuff going on.

How you actually create a newsletter depends on how fancy you'd like it to be and what kind of budget you're operating with. Here are a few user-friendly options:

- **Yahoo! Groups**—http://groups.yahoo.com

  Yahoo! Groups is an easy, tried-and-true way to create email lists. Although most people think of these things as discussion forums where users can reply to the group at large and start conversations, you can easily set up a group to be announce-only and use it to distribute your organization's newsletter. With the site's new Rich Text Editor, you can even include images and hyperlinks. Best of all, it's free.

- **iContact**—http://www.icontact.com

  If you want a little more configurability, more features, a slicker design, and an interface designed specifically with newsletters in mind, iContact might be up your alley. It's $10 per month for lists of up to 250 contacts, $14 per month for lists of up to 500 contacts, and $19 for lists of up to 1,000 contacts (the price scales all the way up to $699/month for lists with more than 100,000 contacts), but nonprofits get a 20% discount. Here's the catch: You can send only a limited number of messages per month through its service—specifically, six times the number of people that constitute your maximum. So if you've subscribed at the minimum rate (up to 250) and you have 250 subscribers, you can send 6 emails per month; if you have 125 subscribers, you can send 12; and so forth.

- **Constant Contact**—http://www.constantcontact.com

  Constant Contact, a competitor to iContact, offers a similar feature set at $15/month for up to 500 contacts and $30/month for up to 2,500 contacts. Unlike iContact, Constant Contact allows you to send an unlimited number of messages per month through its service.

If you are considering a newsletter, you might have some questions right up front:

- **Do you even need a newsletter?**—Maybe. Email newsletters can serve a useful purpose if you have a lot of members who are Internet-engaged enough to do email, but not Internet-engaged enough that they follow you on Facebook or Twitter. Email newsletters aren't as important as they used to be, and I expect they'll be obsolete within five years due to the emergence of more spam-savvy, eye-catching, easy-to-sort social networking and social bookmarking technologies. According to a 2006 study by Jakob Nielsen, only 19% of newsletter subscribers actually read their newsletter from beginning to end. Most of the purposes served by an email newsletter are just as well-served by shorter, less comprehensive email updates that highlight a specific action or fundraising initiative.

- **How many subscribers should you expect?**—That's impossible to gauge for sure in advance, but my experience has been that email newsletter subscriber bases tend to build slowly, proportionate to the membership of the organization.

- **What can you put in a newsletter?**—Anything you want, within reason.

- **What *should* you put in a newsletter?**—Event announcements, articles, and action alerts that involve stuff that people will do within the next two to four weeks. If it's further off than that, you can still mention it in the email newsletter, but odds are good that your audience will forget it by the time the date rolls around, and people don't tend to save emails.

- **Should you use HTML or plain text?**—That depends. Would you rather readers ignore your newsletter because it looks dull or complain about your newsletter because their email client won't display it properly? Most organizations choose door #2, so they go with HTML newsletters. But if your newsletter is simple and text-driven, it may make more sense to do it as plain text and just include URLs rather than HTML links.

- **Should you use pictures?**—Sparingly, if at all. If your newsletter includes more than 50k of graphics, it's a safe bet that it will still load slowly on some computers—and if lots of graphics are inserted as attachments, odds are good that some email servers will bounce the newsletter because it's too big.

- **How many people read their email newsletters?**—There's no reliable data on that. A shrinking number, given the number of emails most people get. I don't usually read mine anymore.

- How many people actually click links in newsletters?—Very, very few. There is no reliable data on just how few.

- **What are some practical disadvantages of using email newsletters?**—They're becoming obsolete, they're inconvenient to read, they're easy to miss and easily mistaken for spam, and they can't be administered in a way that will please more than 75% of your likely readers. Other than that, they're fantastic.

- **So why should you bother?**—Email newsletters can be very useful if you have a lot of members who receive emails but haven't connected to your organization using social media yet, and they're less expensive and easier to produce than print newsletters. But they're not something you probably want to spend a huge amount of your money, time, or resources on because tightly-formatted bulk email is very 1998. If you have to ask yourself whether your organization needs an email newsletter, and members aren't specifically asking for one, it probably doesn't. It's usually best to just sent out individual email notifications about events and actions every so often instead.

Using Twitter

Founded in 2006, Twitter (www.twitter.com) is a giant collective text-messaging conversation that organizations and individuals can use to broadcast messages of up to 140 characters to a group of voluntary readers. In other words, bulk text messaging. Because Twitter "tweets" (messages) can be quickly sent in via cell phone and because they're short enough for everyone to keep up with a large number, its activism implications are pretty huge (see Table 8.1).

Table 8.1—25 Great Twitter Feeds for Activists

Twitter ID		Why You Should Follow
@ACLU	The American Civil Liberties Union	Reports, action alerts, and other info from the nation's leading civil liberties group.
@amnesty	Amnesty International	International human rights organization with a strong online presence.
@change	Change.org	Tweets from one of the largest online activism sites, with regularly-posted updates.
@erintothemax	Erin Matson, VP/Action of the National Organization for Women (NOW)	Advice, action alerts, and general commentary from an innovative e-activist.
@faraichideya	Farai Chideya, media personality and author (*Don't Believe the Hype*, et. al.).	Commentary and links dealing with racial justice, women's rights, poverty, and media.
@feministnews	Feminist Majority Foundation.	Newsfeed from the FMF, which deals with women's issues in the United States and internationally.
@Guttmacher	Guttmacher Institute.	Studies and reports from a leading international organization on sexuality and reproductive justice issues.

Table 8.1—25 Great Twitter Feeds for Activists

Twitter ID		Why You Should Follow
@helenprejean	Sister Helen Prejean of the Order of St. Joseph of Medaille, anti-death penalty activist and author (*Dead Man Walking*, et. al.).	Excellent example of how to run a Twitter feed that both reflects the author's personality and focuses, with discipline, on a single issue.
@Info_Activism	Tactical Technology Collective, an organization "helping human rights advocates use information, communications and digital technologies to maximise the impact of their advocacy work."	It's exactly what it claims to be. If you do e-activism and have a Twitter account, this is a must-follow.
@JamilSmith	Independent film producer and civil rights activist Jamil Smith.	Tweets on race, class, and politics. Low-profile but invaluable, particularly as an aggregator of important activism-related stories you might otherwise miss.
@JoeTrippi	Joe Trippi, pioneering e-activist and manager of Howard Dean's 2004 presidential campaign.	Trippi was one of the first to make large-scale use of the Internet's activism potential and the very first to use it as the basis of a serious national campaign. When he tweets, modern-day e-activists should listen.
@leareiter	Lea Reiter, immigrants' rights activist.	If you follow immigrants' rights issues, Reiter is one of the best voices on how you can put e-activism to the service of the cause.
@mashable	Official Twitter feed of Mashable (www.mashable.com), the leading social media website.	If you use social media (Twitter, Facebook, or any of the sites I've described in Chapter 4, "Engage with Social Networking Sites") to do e-activism, you should follow this site—or at least its Twitter feed—to stay up to date on the latest tricks and technologies.
@NAACP	The NAACP, leading black civil rights organization since 1909.	New NAACP president Ben Jealous has always had an ear for new media, and his administration has made the NAACP an e-activism powerhouse. Follow the Twitter feed to keep up.
@Network4Good	Network for Good (www.networkforgood.com), an online donation-processing website for nonprofits.	NetworkForGood isn't always the most cost-effective way of accepting donations (see Chapter 6, "How to Raise Funds Online"), but the organization's Twitter feed provides a constant stream of helpful e-activism tips and links.

Table 8.1—25 Great Twitter Feeds for Activists

Twitter ID		Why You Should Follow
@NickKristof	*New York Times* columnist Nicholas Kristof, human rights investigative journalist and co-author of *Half the Sky: Turning Oppression Into Opportunity for Women Worldwide* (2009).	An idea leader on international human rights issues, who covers issues all over the political spectrum and links to many e-activism opportunities.
@racialjustice	*ColorLines* (www.colorlines.com), a national magazine covering race issues.	If you only follow one Twitter feed on race in America, make it this one.
@reasonmag	*Reason* (www.reason.com), a high-traffic online libertarian magazine.	Lots of content and occasional action alerts in support of low taxes, free trade, and other fiscally conservative issues.
@SisterSong_WOC	SisterSong, a reproductive justice organization for women of color.	E-activism on race, feminism, and women's health care issues.
@socialcitizen	Kari Saratovsky, VP/Social Innovation at the Case Foundation and all-around expert on e-activism and nonprofits.	Covers the intersection between social media and philanthropy, with a great deal of information that would be of interest to other e-activists as well.
@socialedge	Social Edge (www.socialedge.org), a website for entrepreneurs who specialize in social media.	While tweets tend to assume an audience of for-profit entrepreneur types, most of the information in this feed is just as relevant to e-activists.
@SomalyMam	Somaly Mam, a Cambodian anti-slavery activist.	Tweets about human trafficking, slavery, and other human rights concerns related to slavery. A good example of how one person can use e-activism to keep an issue visible and cover it better than many well-funded organizations do.
@unicefusa	UNICEF, U.S. branch	The official Twitter feed of the U.S. office of the United Nations Children's Fund (UNICEF). Good information on children's issues in the context of global human rights—and a good illustration of how Twitter can be used for fundraising and topic visibility.
@wired	*Wired* magazine (www.wired.com)	Like *Wired* itself, the Twitter feed focuses on and science. Very useful articles for e-activists, particularly those interested in the newest technologies.
@witness.org	WITNESS (www.witness.org), an organization that donates videocameras to document human rights abuses.	An excellent illustration of how Twitter can be used to highlight activist multimedia.

Twitter's power in the activist's world is noteworthy. Just ask James Karl Buck. As CNN reported in 2008:

> "Buck, a graduate student from the University of California-Berkeley, was in Mahalla, Egypt, covering an anti-government protest when he and his translator, Mohammed Maree (see Figure 8.2), were arrested April 10.
>
> On his way to the police station, Buck took out his cell phone and sent a message to his friends and contacts using the micro-blogging site Twitter.
>
> The message only had one word. "Arrested."
>
> Within seconds, colleagues in the United States and his blogger-friends in Egypt—the same ones who had taught him the tool only a week earlier—were alerted that he was being held."

> > > NOTE

To read more, see: "Student 'Twitters' His Way Out of Egyptian Jail," CNN.com, www.cnn.com/2008/TECH/04/25/twitter.buck"

Buck was released after less than 24 hours, but Maree was held for several months. The fact that Buck was American probably helped, but the fact that his arrest so quickly became public knowledge couldn't have hurt either.

Twitter was also used by on-the-ground activists during the Iranian elections protests of 2009, where they used it to provide an account that the state-run media operating in the Iranian closed society would not have been able to provide.

Although your organization's or cause's use of Twitter might not be quite *that* dramatic, it can be a useful tool to promote new links, highlight breaking news, call for action, and build relationships with supporters.

Is Direct Bulk SMS Messaging Becoming Obsolete?

A few years ago, bulk SMS/MMS text messaging was the big thing for event announcements—users could subscribe to an SMS list and get updates on their cell phone instantly. The Barack Obama 2008 presidential campaign famously used one of these not only to update users on events and fundraising initiatives, but also to take polls and announce the outcome of primaries and caucuses.

Several practical problems exist with direct bulk SMS messaging, though: It can cost money for the recipients, it always costs money for the sender (sometimes a prohibitively large amount of money), and it's been replaced by cheaper, easier-to-use sites, such as Facebook and Twitter, which now allow users to receive new status updates as SMS messages.

Direct bulk SMS as an activism tool took a long time to catch on, but I don't think it's sticking around. It fills a brief window between the mass adoption of SMS as a messaging platform and the mass adoption of cheaper, more convenient alternatives to direct bulk SMS. Personally, I wouldn't put a lot of money, or time, into it. Even now, it presents few practical advantages over Twitter.

Figure 8.2
Mohammed Maree. Photo: © 2008 James Buck. Licensed under Creative Commons Attribution License 2.0 Generic.

If you are just getting started with Twitter (or are considering a Twitter account) following are answers to some questions you might have.

- **Do you or your organization really need a Twitter account?**—Probably not, but it doesn't hurt. Twitter—microblogging in general, really—represents a new way to distribute information and links in little soundbites to large numbers of people. Or occasionally small numbers of people.

- **How many Twitter followers do you need?**—That depends on the objectives and scope of your organization. If you're dealing with a local organization, a dozen followers—if they're active and would be interested in the information—could be enough. But you can never really have too many.

- **How can you get more followers?**—By producing long-term, high-quality tweets. There are various advertising gimmicks you can use, and it's always possible to follow auto-follower Twitter bots that will artificially inflate your follower count, but for the most part this doesn't serve the interests of activism. The important thing is to make sure that everybody who is likely to want to subscribe to your Twitter feed knows it exists—by publicizing it through other media associated with your organization and by linking to it from other online content. A high follower count, in and of itself, isn't necessarily helpful.

- **How often should you tweet?**—According to Dan Zarrella at HubSpot, the most high-traffic Twitter streams contain between 10 and 50 tweets per day, with 22 as an optimum. But unless you're trying to become one of the most high-traffic Twitter streams out there, that's a very flexible rule. It's probably optimal to (except for replies) tweet no more often than once every 30 minutes or so, and no less often than once every 18 hours or so—but if it makes sense to you to do otherwise, go with your gut.

- **What should you say in your tweets?**—You should make them as conversational and entertaining as possible, while still conveying the message and any essential links. Let's say you're trying to promote an action alert protesting the defeat of a proposed international ban on the fishing of bluefin tuna, an endangered species commonly harvested for sushi. A lot of tweeters might use the actual title of the action alert with the URL, e.g.:

Bluefin Tuna Harvesting Ban Defeated. http://www.bluefin.url/39282

But that looks like spam; it doesn't look like a human being wrote it. Compare it to:

We can revive the bluefin tuna harvesting ban. Take action here: http://www.bluefin.url/39282

The important thing is to look like you're having a conversation with your readers. If you don't, they're not going to feel engaged. And Twitter is an interactive medium.

- **How many of your tweets should include links?**—No more than one-third, ideally. The rest of the Internet is full of hyperlinked content; Twitter is supposed to read more like a conversation. That said: In practice, most nonprofit organizations primarily tweet links. (Most celebrities, on the other hand, do not—and they get a lot more followers.)

- **So what should the other two-thirds of your tweets contain?**—Anything you want, within reason. If you're tweeting on a specific topic, keep it relevant to that topic and try to post things that you think many of your readers might actually want to read.

- **What if I can't come up with anything remotely interesting to say?**—Then it's probably better to just tweet links.

- **Given that Twitter is interactive, do you need to reply to every tweet somebody sends you?**—If you're being asked a serious question to which you know the answer, usually. If it's a helpful or complimentary comment about your work or your organization's work, a thank-you never hurts but is generally optional. If it's a snarky comment, unfair criticism, or anything else that looks like a waste of time, ignore it.

- **Should you use software that will automatically post your blog entries as tweets?**—You can, but I don't really recommend it. I personally tend to unfollow Twitter users whose tweets all look auto-generated; they're tedious to read, and it's not immediately clear which links I want to follow and which links I don't. The human connection is key, and that generally requires a human author.

Blogging

Most individual web pages are like whiteboard. You put what you want on it, and when you want to change something, you erase the old and add in the new. You can have as many whiteboards as you want, and they can refer to each other, but each of them stands alone, from the reader's point of view, as independent pieces of content.

Blogs (short for "web logs" because originally that's what they were—logs, journals) tend to be read differently. They're presented in reverse chronological order and are more-or-less endless. The newest is up top, and then you keep reading and there's the second newest, the third newest, the fourth, and so on. When the page gets too long, the oldest cycles out of display into an archive, automatically by way of the blogging software, as the newest are added at the top. Unless you have made a serious typo or accidentally defamed somebody or made some other error of content, blog posts aren't really meant to be revised; that's why they have dates on them. They send the implicit message of a work in progress.

There's something else special about blogs, too: nearly all of them allow user comments in a special Comments field underneath each post, where readers can pipe in with their own points of view on their own discussion pages without disrupting the appearance of the blog itself. Blogs were the first real part of what is now called Web 2.0—the participatory Internet, where most web pages allow some kind of two-way conversation to take place.

Blogs are such a great idea that everybody thinks they need one, and quite often they don't. You should not maintain a blog, for starters, unless you're really interested in writing content for it often enough to keep it relatively fresh. If I go to a regular website that hasn't been updated since 2007, I might or might not know it. If I go to a blog that hasn't been updated since 2007, it shows its age because the date of the most recent post sits there looking at me like the frame of an old abandoned house.

However, if you're interested in writing for a blog and/or can get other people interested in writing for a blog (many blogs have multiple authors), it can be a worthwhile tool for activism.

The most popular blog-design sites are WordPress (www.wordpress.com) and Blogspot (www.blogspot.com). Both are free, and both make the technical side of things a nonissue. Just provide the sites with your server information and tell it where you want it to stick the blog, fill out the various forms associated with how you want your blog to look, and you're set. You can install server-side software if you want to get really fancy, but there's not necessarily any real need—for most purposes, you can run WordPress without installing it on your server just as easily.

Blogging is big business, as shown in Figure 8.3.

If you are considering a blog for your activism purposes, you will want to consider the following:

* **Does your organization or cause need a blog?**—Yes, if there are people who really want to write one or who are paid reasonably well to do so. But there's an old Internet maxim: Don't build what you can't maintain. You can't have an up-to-date blog if you don't have one or more dedicated bloggers. This means passion in the case of a volunteer or good compensation in the case of a staffer or contractor. Don't make the mistake of just assigning a blog to somebody who already has a full calendar, with no additional compensation. Newspapers did this during a recent recession, and the end result has for the most part been a lot of dormant (or really poorly-written) newspaper blogs. Good blogs take time, commitment, and—I believe—usually at least a little bit of passion. Blog writing, like every other kind of writing, requires real work and a certain amount of skill.

Figure 8.3
The lobby at Blog World Expo. Photo: © 2008 Shashi Bellamkonda. Licensed under Creative Commons Attribution License 2.0 Generic.

- **How often should you post blog entries?**—That's a question that only you and your readers can answer, and you can only answer it after the blog has been around long enough to develop a reader base. As long as you don't go more than two weeks between posts or miss a major development relevant to your organization, you're probably doing fine. There's not really any such thing as blogging too frequently, but blogging more than once in the same 24-hour period, unless there's something really big going on that you're blogging about in real time, is probably not a good use of your energy.

- **How long should blog posts be?**—I've served as About.com's Guide to Civil Liberties (http://civilliberty.about.com) since early 2006, and one of the components of that site is a blog. One thing I've learned over the past four years as site guide is that blogs don't make a good long-form medium. If your blog post is consistently high-quality and runs to more than 400 words, you set a standard for yourself that becomes very difficult to meet on a regular basis—and readers expect a regularly-updated blog. I personally believe that you should go for short. 5-7 paragraphs per post, max. Anything longer than that, and it should probably be published as an op-ed in your local newspaper. (Or as a freestanding article on your website.) There are exceptions to this rule, and one of them is DailyKos (http://www.dailykos.com), an extremely active political blog that practically defines left-wing politics in the Internet age. Bloggers on that site can go on for thousands and thousands of words, and that's what readers have come to expect from it—and it has enough contributors that maintaining that level of productivity isn't a problem. But even if you have enough contributors, short, pithy, frequent blog posts are what people generally expect.

- **How can you get more readers?**—Keep writing high-quality posts on a consistent basis, and odds are very good that your readership will steadily increase. Be sure to list your blog in Technorati (http://www.technorati.com) and tell other bloggers who write on your topic the first time you crosslink their work (which will also let them know that you exist). There is no quick, reliable method to dramatically increasing your readership. Sometimes it happens quickly, but that's usually more of an accident than anything else.

Your E-Activism Toolkit: Keeping Allies in the Loop

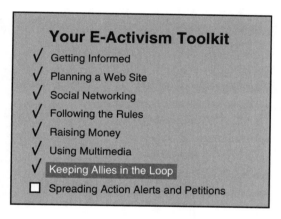

Sustainability. Diligence. Staying power. Keeping activists engaged can be hard work, but the first step is keeping them informed somehow, in some way. Let me give you an example that springs to mind because it just happened recently, and it's an excellent cautionary tale.

Over the spring, I got interested in an activist organization with which I've had a friendly but fairly distant relationship. I was under the impression, based on what I had heard from some colleagues who were involved in the group, that they held regular meetings. I emailed several officers asking for information on these meetings. Only one officer replied, and she indicated that she wasn't sure when the next meeting would be. Other organizations contacted me asking me for my time (I'm an elected officer in several; it happens), so I got distracted.

Earlier this week—on Wednesday, it's important—I received a form email from the organization's president letting me know that the group's annual meeting would be held Saturday morning at 11 a.m. at a location more than an hour's drive away and asking me to contribute funds. I'm already booked for Saturday with another activism-related event, and I'm disinclined to spend my hard-earned money on an organization when I can't figure out what it actually does.

That's the bottom line: It doesn't really matter how important your organization is, and it doesn't really matter how important your cause is. If you can't put me to work, I'm moving on.

That's one activist's perspective.

Action Alerts and Online Petitions

"A lot of people are waiting for Martin Luther King or Mahatma Gandhi to come back—but they are gone. We are it. It is up to us. It is up to you."

—Marian Wright Edelman

The old aphorism that actions speak louder than words is a pretty painful thing to hear when you're dealing with a medium that's made up mainly of words. But words *can* be actions if you hone them down to a sharp edge and point them in the right direction.

To quote the great American philosopher Cher: "Words are like weapons; / they wound sometimes." On my desk I keep a little Nepali statue of the Tibetan Buddhist bodhisattva Manjushri, the patron saint of philosophers. In his right hand, he carries a flame-tipped sword. The sword isn't for combat or any violent purpose—the battlefield is no place for philosophy, and violence is an unsuitable occupation for a Buddhist saint—rather, it is an icon referred to as the sword of discriminating wisdom. Manjushri's job is to slice through lies and unclear thinking, to suggest practices that will relieve human suffering. So is ours.

It's hard, the way online activism relies so much on words. But words can produce more words, and those words more words still, and enough words—carefully chosen and targeted in the right places—can change the world. They often have. See Figure 9.1. Constitutions, declarations of independence and of war, influential novels and works of political philosophy, the Bible, the Qur'an, *The Origin of Species, The Feminist Mystique, Silent Spring,* every piece of legislation that has ever been passed, voted down, or vetoed—these are all made of words.

Figure 9.1
Martin Luther King Jr. (left) converses with Malcolm X (right). The words of King and Malcolm repre-
sented different elements of the civil rights movement—King representing unity, Malcolm repre-
senting black solidarity—but both figures were likely essential to its success. Photo: Library of
Congress.

Writing Effective Action Alerts

An action alert is any email or web page that calls on a user to contact legislators or other
decision makers to express their views on a given issue or to take other action to influence a
developing event. Some are web forms that users can fill out to automatically send messages
to decision makers; others ask users to take initiative themselves by sending an email, making
a phone call, or mailing a letter.

The latter approach is easier to implement (all you have to do is write an ordinary message
that can be distributed as an email or put up on a web page and social networks), easier to
distribute (people can cut-and-paste the content of action alerts into emails and send them
along to friends), and, by and large, less expensive. But web forms are easier to *use* and might
be a more effective approach if you're looking for a large number of responses.

The drawback of web forms is that they require some web programming know-how, and full-
featured online action alerts generally require the use of an expensive professional online
grassroots lobbying service such as Capitol Advantage's CapWiz (www.capitoladvantage/cap-
wiz), which can be prohibitively expensive.

Who is a Decisionmaker?

Conventional wisdom says that action alerts should be addressed to elected officials. Most are, but don't let that limit your options.

Let's imagine, for example, that a local catering business publishes an offensive advertisement in the newspaper. Relevant organizations in this situation might include the business itself, the advertising agency, the newspaper, or government agencies and nonprofits that use the catering business; relevant decisionmakers at these organizations would be appropriate subjects of an action alert campaign.

But choosing the right decisionmaker can be tricky. Going directly to the catering business's clients would be the most brutal approach and not necessarily the most effective. A better outcome might be to identify the person in charge of making advertising-related decisions at the catering business and use an action alert campaign to get them to print a written apology and take the advertisement out of circulation.

Whatever kind of action alert you create, remember:

- **A happy ending is best**—Before you send out an action alert, you should always have a desired outcome in mind—something specific that you expect the action alert to accomplish and something that is within the power of the decisionmaker to accomplish.

- **Do your homework**—In fact, it's generally best if you contact the decisionmaker yourself before you've put out the action alert to make sure they aren't already on your side. (But don't threaten to send an Internet action alert; they'll probably laugh at you. Most decisionmakers haven't fully absorbed the potential impact of these things yet.) If the person agrees to do what your action alert requests, right away, then there's no need for an action alert. An action alert should not be a decisionmaker's first opportunity to learn that something needs to be done.

- **It matters who you contact**—And it's hard to know sometimes. When in doubt, choose the person with the most direct influence over the situation. For example: if you want to see local criminal charges dropped, the first line of action is to contact the local district attorney, not the state (or, worse, U.S.) attorney general.

- **It matters how you contact them**—Experienced grassroots lobbyists have told me that the most effective way to influence policymakers is to talk to them face to face, both because it forces them to interact with you on a human level and because it shows them that you care enough about the issue to actually show up. The second most effective way is to send a letter; it gives them a material object that they have to throw away or file (see Figure 9.2), and it shows that you care enough to write a letter and pay postage. The third most effective way is to call, and the least effective way is to only contact the policymaker electronically (though email is far more effective than an e-petition, especially if the decisionmaker is an elected official and you're a constituent). At the very least, your action alert should include the work number of the policymaker you're trying to reach.

- **It matters what you say**—Make sure the action alert includes good talking points.

- **Inaccuracies sabotage an action alert**—So check your facts.

- **A panicked tone reduces the credibility of an action alert**—So keep the dire warnings and exclamation points to a minimum. If it's all that bad, you won't have to build it up—the facts will speak for themselves.

- **The audience is the most important ingredient**—So distribute the action alert to media and to groups that you believe are likely to have a large number of sympathetic participants. Put it on your group's web page and put it on your group's social networking page.

- **This doesn't justify a captive audience**—If you keep an email distribution list for action alerts, make sure that you honor requests to be removed from that email distribution list.

Figure 9.2

One of the benefits of printed flyers and other activist material is that it's a physical object that visibly takes up space and has to be stored, given away, or discarded. Some voters will keep a copy of this Obama flyer and map, held by a volunteer, for many years to come. Photo: © 2008 Dennis Crowley. Licensed under Creative Commons Attribution License 2.0 Generic.

Good action alerts should include the following:

- The name of the sponsoring organization, with a phone number and web URL.

- A paragraph or two describing the crisis.

- A short statement indicating how the person(s) being contacted can resolve the crisis and why they should.

- Contact information for the person(s) in question.

In mid-2009, I distributed an action alert protesting a prominent Mississippi state senator's decision to keynote the annual conference of a white supremacist organization:

(from Tom Head's Mississippi Human Rights Report, http://www.mississippihumanrightsreport.net)

WHITE SEPARATISM IN THE MISSISSIPPI STATE SENATE?

July 5, 2009

Last weekend, Sen. Lydia Chassaniol (R-Winona) was the keynote speaker at the annual convention of the Council of Conservative Citizens, an organization that has been classified as a white separatist hate group by the Southern Poverty Law Center and described as having "a thinly-veiled white supremacist agenda" by *The New York Times*. On the CCC web site, you can buy a "white pride" T-shirt; their platform praises America's "European" heritage and condemns "mixture of the races"; a previous incarnation of their web site described African Americans as "a retrograde species of humanity"; and so forth. The organization's agenda is fairly transparent.

Sen. Chassaniol has refused to disavow the organization, praising it as a group of "lone voices crying in the wilderness" during her keynote and stating that its presence "gives [her] hope." When she was later asked about her membership in the group, she replied that "a person's membership in any organization is a private matter."

Why should we care? Several reasons:

Sen. Chassaniol chairs the Mississippi Senate Tourism Committee, and arguably wields more power than any other legislator to shape how Mississippi is perceived by non-residents.

Sen. Chassaniol is one of the most visible Republicans in the state, even independently of her role on the tourism committee. She is a popular speaker at conservative events, and has *her own blog* on the *Clarion-Ledger* website. Watching her sacrifice her credibility to support this unworthy organization is tragic.

The last mainstream Republican politician to openly support the Council of Conservative Citizens was Governor Kirk Fordice in the 1990s. Former RNC Chair Jim Nicholson, Governor Haley Barbour, Senator Trent Lott (who condemned the group as "white supremacist and racist"), and former Jackson City Council President Ben Allen have all spoken out against the organization—Republican politicians, in other words, at every level of government. Sen. Chassaniol's participation in the annual CofCC convention gives them the undeserved opportunity to reenter the mainstream of Republican politics in Mississippi.

Mississippians need Sen. Chassaniol to admit that she seriously misjudged the organization.

Action Items

Leave a message for Sen. Lydia Chassaniol at (601) 359 3226 politely but firmly asking her to cancel her membership with the Council of Conservative Citizens and publicly apologize for speaking at their convention.

Leave a message for Mississippi RNC Chair Brad White at (601) 948 5191 requesting that he reaffirm former RNC Chair Jim Nicholson's rejection of the Council of Conservative

Citizens, so that no statewide politicians get the wrong idea from Sen. Chassaniol's partic-ipation in the event (given her high level of visibility in the Mississippi Republican Party). The party of James Meredith and Charles Evers does not need to be associated with seg-regationist ideology.

At the end, I included links on further information pertaining to the group. It did stir up public sentiment surrounding the issue—my subsequent open letter on the issue was published in the local alternative weekly, and I even ended up giving a 50-minute radio interview about it on a statewide talk radio show. Although neither the senator nor the party chair apologized or meaningfully denounced the group, the action alert was effective to the extent that it drew public attention to the issue.

Break the Chain

You know those annoying email chain letters that appeal to readers' good intentions but get the facts com-pletely wrong and suggest a course of action that will do no good for anybody?

They're your competition.

I used to be known as the jerk who replied to chain-letter senders—sending replies with links to the rele-vant pages on www.snopes.com (The Urban Legend Reference Pages) and http://urbanlegends.about.com (About.com: Urban Legends)—but there was a method to my madness and still is. Flaky email chain letters are *counterfeit activism*.

The problem with counterfeit currency is that it deprives businesses of real income by instead giving some-thing that only *looks* real, and that it devalues legitimate currency by flooding the market with stuff that isn't actually worth anything.

Phony email chain letters work in the same way. Send one and you *think* you've done something good, and if you fell for the ruse you get the same warm fuzzies you'd get if you'd done something really useful, like fired off a short letter to your legislator or made a small donation to a legitimate charity.

As activists, we don't want a monopoly on those warm fuzzies. But we don't want hucksters to go around stealing them out from under our noses, either.

Please, go ahead and be the jerk who tells people the email chain letters are phony. But be nice about it.

Are Massive Online Petitions a Waste of Time?

Barbara Mikkelson of Snopes (www.snopes.com), the urban legends reference site, put it harshly but probably put it best:

"Paper-and-ink petitions are signed in a variety of handwriting styles, each unique to its signer. Consequently, signatures on a paper-and-ink petition cannot easily be faked else certain glaring similarities would show up in one entry after another.

E-petitions, however, come with no such assurance—the same person could have generated all of the signatures. Moreover, it takes little by way of programming skills to create a sequence of code that will randomly generate fake names, e-mail addresses, and cities...

Those in a position to influence anything know this and thus accord e-petitions only slightly more respect than they would a blank sheet of paper."

> > > N O T E

See "Internet Petitions," by Barbara Mikkelson at Snopes.com, www.snopes.com/inboxer/petition/internet.asp.

I don't know if I'd go quite *that* far—many credible e-petition sites require email verification, and it's not so easy to create thousands of email addresses, from different domains, out of whole cloth—but as a practical matter, large e-petitions are far less effective than traditional pen-and-ink petitions (see Figure 9.3) and may be the least effective way to communicate protest. The numbers sound impressive in terms of how widespread a sentiment might be, how well-promoted a petition might be, but they indicate so little action on the part of the signer that they don't necessarily show any real depth of commitment to the position being advocated. They're not quite "click a button if you agree," but they're close.

Figure 9.3
An Ohio activist signs a print petition for workers' rights legislation. Photo: © 2008 Bernard Pollack. Licensed under Creative Commons Attribution License 2.0 Generic.

Action alerts are better. If someone doesn't care enough about an issue to fire off an email or make a phone call, policymakers don't necessarily care what that person's opinion on the matter is because it's unlikely to affect the larger culture or reduce their level of support.

However, there are things you can do to make e-petitions more useful than they might other-wise be:

- As a general rule, the more information you ask for and provide, the more credible the petition. An e-petition with names and validated email addresses is better than an e-petition without validated email addresses; an e-petition with all of the above, plus city and state, is even better.

- *Where* an e-petition goes is as important as, or more important than, any other factor. E-petitions addressed to the President of the United States, for example, are seldom useful because the President is lobbied on so many issues that e-petitions are likely to get lost in the shuffle. As with action alerts, focus your attention on the lowest-ranked person with the power to change things.

- If you can, ask permission in the petition to reuse email addresses provided in the petition for future, related activism efforts.

- Creative use of e-petitions can be beneficial. Remember the action alert I described above? Another local activist, Beth Kander, appended the names of nearly 100 people (with their permission) to a joint letter opposing the keynote, which she then hand-delivered as a gift note, with flowers, to Sen. Chassaniol's office. The people were locals; Sen. Chassaniol had very likely met at least a few of them; and their identity was easy enough to verify, in any case, that it would not have been realistic for anyone to suspect that the names would have been faked. Sen. Chassaniol still never apologized, but if anything would have done the trick, I think it would have been Beth's flowers.

Why Is This Page Black?

On February 8th, 1996, President Bill Clinton signed the Telecommunications Act of 1996 into law. Included as Title V was the Communications Decency Act, legislation that would impose up to a two-year prison sentence on anyone who...knowingly (A) uses an interactive computer service to send to a specific person or persons under 18 years of age, or (B) **uses any interactive computer service to display in a manner available to a person under 18 years of age,** any comment, request, suggestion, proposal, image, or other communication that, in context, depicts or describes, in terms patently offensive as measured by contemporary community standards, sexual or excretory activities or organs.

In practice, this would have meant no profanity, nudity, or indecent content of any kind on web pages or other publicly available Internet location, or in any material provided over the Internet to anyone whose age had not been verified by the sender. The policy would have actually been far more aggressive than the FCC's anti-indecency provisions, which level fines against broadcasters but do not involve prison sentences.

The Voters Telecommunications Watch, an organization made up of Internet civil rights activists working alongside the Electronic Frontier Foundation (EFF) to fight the legislation, held a protest for two days—on February 8th and 9th—asking that website authors temporarily turn their page backgrounds black in protest against the bill and link to a website explaining why this had been done.

The statute was never enforced, pending judicial review, and was officially struck down by the Supreme Court in *ACLU v. Reno* (1997).

Similar campaigns since then have often centered on social networking profile pictures (one campaign calling on supporters to turn their pictures green in solidarity with Iranian human rights activists), status updates, and other means that Internet users can use to demonstrate their views on a given issue. This sort of thing is useful inasmuch as it affects the online culture around a policy issue, and there will no doubt be much, much more of it.

Your E-Activism Toolkit: Action Alerts and Petitions

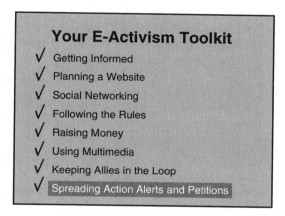

When the United States was first founded, the right to petition elected officials was seen as so important that it was explicitly included in the First Amendment. Today, petitions aren't such a big deal. What changed?

Travel and media. In 1790, getting a group together to sign a document—as the Declaration of Independence had been signed a generation before—was a major undertaking, one that would involve considerable inconvenience and expense. And the country was so small and so new that it was conceivable that the same names would have kept showing up on petitions—the same cranks, very much like the Founding Fathers once were.

But now that any person can sign an e-petition and do so with any amount of effort, it means less that someone has done it. Policymakers are impressed by views that are strongly held and widespread. Views that are weakly held and widespread, or strongly held and marginal, don't tend to concern them much.

It's hard work, all of this, and at times most online activism feels a little ineffective, even a little counterfeit. Is it? Where does online activism fit into the broader context of activism in the United States?

Follow me into the next chapter, and we'll discuss it.

It's Your World, So Change It

"We shape our tools and thereafter our tools shape us."

—Marshall McLuhan

I was in a friend's passenger seat on the way home from the Mississippi State Capitol in early 2007, and we started talking about some e-petitions that people had filled out in lieu of calling local legislators. We were frustrated. My friend is young, but she's an old-school community organizer; right now she's organizing for the rights of low-income Miami residents, and at the time she was president of the Jackson chapter of the National Organization for Women (NOW). For my part, I was relatively new to activism but very much focused on *getting stuff done,* and I could see that most of what people did online that they referred to as activism seemed to be more about feeling good than doing good.

"Tom," she told me, "e-activism is killing *real* activism."

That sentiment was echoed in a May 2009 article by Georgetown diplomacy scholar Evgeny Morozov, who wrote in "The Brave New World of Slacktivism"

> "Perhaps, it's high time to challenge this narrative and ask a very difficult question: Are the publicity gains gained through this greater reliance on new media worth the organizational losses that traditional activists entities are likely to suffer, as ordinary people would begin to turn away from conventional (and proven) forms of activism (demonstrations, sit-ins, confrontation with police, strategic litigation, and so on) and embrace more 'slacktivist' forms, which may be more secure but whose effectiveness is still largely unproven?"

The only way I can think of to answer Morozov's question is by looking at the history of other media that changed activism, and the manner in which they were incorporated—or not—into "real" activism.

Online activism is a great *tool*, and there's even a place in most movements for people who don't do anything else—which is fantastic because there are people who really *can't* do anything else who are brought into the process and given ways to get stuff accomplished by way of online activism. So don't take this as an indication that there's anything wrong with doing only online work. There isn't; it's as important as any other medium and more important than most.

But imagine if activists looked at any other medium or activism device the way they so often look at the Internet. Nobody on a tight budget would casually print 300 flyers and just leave them on their desk, but people create and pay for websites all the time that they don't actually promote or use. Nobody with sense would pay a lobbyist a yearly salary and then perform no evaluation of any kind with respect to how well the lobbyist performs his or her duties.

Online activism has the reputation of being a medium that basically does its own work—low cost, high rewards—when in reality online activism usually takes steady, disciplined work and has to be integrated with more traditional forms of activism in order to build a large, influential movement. Online activism also has to be done by people who are interested in committing time and energy to it. It has a lower overhead than other media, and the workload for online activism can be easily distributed among enough people that it does not become burdensome, but online activism is not a perpetual motion machine.

Most activist groups seem to realize this, but every now and then you'll still hear people, even staffers at well-respected national organizations, talk about how the solution to one problem or another is to make more use of the Internet. But it's not enough to "make more use of the Internet"; you have to have an idea of what, specifically, you're going to use the Internet to do.

E-activism will harm traditional activism if, and only if, it is not incorporated into traditional activism. Fortunately, while there is reason for concern, there is also reason for hope: History is replete with examples of technology that posed a similar threat at first but later became traditional activism tools.

How the Internet Is Like Air Travel

In 1893, author and journalist Julian Hawthorne speculated on the role that air travel might play in the development of American political life. Looking ahead a century to the year 1993, here's what he came up with:

> The main difference between life now (1993), and as it was in your day (1893), is that ours is comparatively an interior, and therefore a more real and absorbing life. For the first time in history we have a real human society. You had the imitation—the symbol—but not the true thing itself.
>
> You will admit that in a perfectly free state man will inevitably select that environment and those companions with which he feels himself most in sympathy—where he finds himself most at home. Now, the power of flight, combined with the modification of the old political conditions that I have mentioned, gave to man this ability to live where and with whom he would. The perfect result could not be attained at once, as it might be in a purely spiritual state; but the tendency was present and the issue was only a question of time.

By degrees, the individuals throughout the world who by mind and temperament were suited to one another, found one another out, and chose habitations where they might be readily accessible to one another. Thus, each family lives in the midst of a circle of families comprising those who are most nearly of one with it in sentiment and quality, and the intercourse of this group is mainly confined to itself.

The same concern has been expressed with respect to the Internet and its potential to divide people—by allowing people with similar views to congregate in forums where they can support each other and ensure that their views, however strange or implausible, are not challenged. As student journalist Lauren Theurer put it ("The Web: Forming Genuine Discourses or Echo Chambers?" *The Mount Holyoke News*, April 15, 2010): "A true downside to the Internet's use for political action is its reinforcement of echo chambers."

Four Offline Technologies That Changed Activism

The Internet is a revolutionary invention, and it changes *everything*, but it isn't the first revolutionary invention to change everything.

The Printing Press

Europe of the fifteenth century was illiterate in part because until there was a way to mass-produce text, there was less incentive to mass-produce literacy. Cambridge University had only 122 books in 1424, and that was an impressively sized library by the standards of the era (though some Chinese libraries had as many as 4,000 books). The invention of the printing press by Johannes Gutenberg in 1440 didn't change everything overnight, but gradual improvements in printer technology later in the century and in subsequent centuries made text cheaper and more accessible.

The Internet is a lot like the printing press in that respect, actually, because it's all about reducing the cost of mass-distributed content. There aren't any reliable statistics on the literacy rate in fifteenth-century Europe, but the only people who really needed to read were clergy, so they were more often than not the only people who were taught how. The vast majority of clergy didn't even own their own Bibles; it would have cost too much. The literacy rate rose when there was enough easily available printed material—most notably, the growth of major newspapers in the eighteenth and nineteenth centuries—to make it worthwhile.

The Internet has comparably affected the rate of personal computer ownership. According to the U.S. Bureau of Labor Statistics, only 15% of Americans owned a computer in 1990. As the Internet began to catch on, the number rose dramatically to 35% by 1997 and, according to a study by the hardware manufacturer Seagate, to 76% by 2005. Not that the Internet is the only reason to purchase a computer, but it has transformed computer access from a luxury to a practical necessity—just as advancements in printing transformed literacy from a luxury to a practical necessity.

The printing press has played a central role in activism almost since its inception, but the United States might have been the first country to be founded as a direct result of printed materials. Thomas Paine's pamphlet *Common Sense* (1776) provided the ideological framework for the American Revolution, and the Federalist Papers (which were essentially 85 printed blog entries written by a few pseudonymous Founding Fathers) established the broad outline of the philosophy behind what would become the U.S. Constitution. Later, unfavorable newspaper coverage would inspire President John Adams to outlaw unsubstantiated criticisms of government officials in 1798, bringing about a backlash that helped to destroy the Federalist Party two years later and gradually move the country toward the bipartisan Democratic-Republican system that we have today. Antislavery newspapers such as William Lloyd Garrison's *The Liberator* and Elijah P. Lovejoy's *Alton Observer* built up Northern opposition to slavery, as did publication of slave memoirs such as *A Narrative of the Life of Frederick Douglass* (1845) and Harriet Jacobs' *Incidents in the Life of a Slave Girl* (1861). And the publication of books, newspapers, and tracts became more influential, and more diverse, during the twentieth century. Now every major activism organization has printed materials; that comes with the territory. And even with the Internet, and the powerful online-only organizations that have begun to emerge, you won't find a complete ideological movement that doesn't have some printed text behind it.

But you're also not going to find a complete ideological movement that consists *entirely* of printed text. Sure, some organizations—worthwhile organizations—do nothing to speak of but research, write, and distribute printed materials, and some individuals focus their activism entirely on researching, writing, and distributing printed materials. Some of them, like Elijah P. Lovejoy (see Figure 10.1), gave their lives for it. But the movement also attracts people who are drawn to other forms of activism: community organizing, grassroots lobbying, action/protest organizing, fundraising, litigation, and so on. And those forms of activism go back millennia.

Figure 10.1
Woodcarving of the burning of Elijah Lovejoy's newspaper headquarters in Alton, Illinois, in November 1837, during a riot in which Lovejoy was ultimately lynched. Public domain. Image courtesy Wikimedia Commons.

Until the Internet came about, no invention had done more to contribute to the spread of ideas and information than the printing press. But even the printing press didn't replace traditional activism; it enhanced it. It was incorporated into it as a tool. You're not likely to see a book on how to use the power of the print medium to change your world because it has already been so completely absorbed into the activist modus operandi. Online activism will be, too, in time.

Telegraphs: The Forgotten Global Network

On October 31, 1902, the first Transpacific telegraph line went live, and the major industrialized cities of the world were linked up in a single electrical communications network.

Telegrams were the nineteenth- and early twentieth-century equivalent to emails; they were short messages sent on devices called telegraphs remotely and far more quickly than mail carriers would allow. This was sometimes useful for activists, for obvious reasons, especially activists focusing on national or international issues.

Perhaps the most crucial activism-related use of the telegraph came about on October 31, 1864, as abolitionists and other supporters of President Abraham Lincoln telegraphed the entire Constitution of Nevada to Washington, DC eight days before the presidential election, allowing Nevada's votes to be counted and increasing Lincoln's margin of victory over challenger George McClellan.

At the time, McClellan—who favored a truce with the Confederacy, and whose more overtly racist supporters feared that the abolition of slavery might result in large-scale "miscenegation" (interracial relationships)—was considered a viable threat. Lincoln ended up winning by a landslide, carrying 55% of the popular vote and all but 21 electoral votes, but in a closer election Nevada's role could have been decisive.

The Telephone

The telephone is something of a mysterious contraption because, by its very nature, it doesn't leave a paper trail. Nobody's entirely sure who invented it first, and nobody can really cite what its first use in an activism context was. But the first organization to really make use of the telephone for large-scale canvassing was probably the Anti-Saloon League in the early 1920s, which rang up people throughout California in an effort to build up regional support.

Today, telephone canvassing is an essential part of political campaigns at every level (see Figure 10.2), and incoming telephone lines, whether operated by volunteers or staff, are essential to all but the most virtual of activist organizations. There are general principles on effective ways to use the telephone for activism, but the phrase "telephone activism" doesn't exactly sound natural. It might have sounded more so in the 1920s.

Telephones are a good example of technology that has been used to build other technology. The Internet as we know it could not exist without telephone lines, and neither could text messaging. Telephones, and their near-ubiquity, made all of this possible.

Figure 10.2
A volunteer in Milwaukee, Wisconsin, phone banks for the 2008 Obama presidential campaign.
Photo: © 2008 Bernard Pollack. Licensed under Creative Commons Attribution License 2.0 Generic.

The Radio

In 1933, the President's Research Committee on Social Trends released a collection of mono-graphs titled *Recent Social Trends in the United States.* The hot new technology of the time, the Internet of that era, was the radio, and the report identified 150 areas in which the radio had significantly affected modern life. Of these, 25 were specifically political—and most would apply to the Internet today just as much as they applied to radio in 1933:

EFFECTS OF THE RADIO TELEGRAPH AND TELEPHONE AND OF RADIO BROADCASTING

IX. ON GOVERNMENT AND POLITICS

- In government, a new regulatory function necessitated.

- Censorship problem raised because of charges of swearing, etc.

- Legal questions raised beginning with the right to air.

- New specialization in law; four air law journals existing.

- New problem of copyright have[sic] arisen.

- New associations created, some active in lobbying.

- Executive pressure on legislatures, through radio appeals.

- A democratizing agency, since political programs and speeches are designed to reach wide varieties of persons at one time.

- Public sentiment aroused in cases of emergencies like drought.

- International affairs affected because of multiplication of national contacts.

- Rumors and propaganda on nationalism have been spread.

- Limits in broadcasting bands foster international arrangements.

- Communication facilitated among belligerents in warfare.

- Procedures of the [political party] nominating conventions altered some-what.

- Constituencies are kept in touch with nominating conventions.

- Political campaigners reach larger audiences.

- The importance of the political mass meeting diminished.

- Presidential "barn-storming" and front porch campaign changed.

- Nature of campaign costs affected.

- Appeal to prejudice of local group lessened.

- Campaign speeches tend to be more logical and cogent.

- An aid in raising campaign funds.

- Campaign speaking by a number of party leaders lessened.

- Campaign promises over radio said to be more binding.

- High government officers who broadcast are said to appear to public less distant and more familiar.

> > > N O T E

See "The Influence of Invention and Discovery," Vol 1, pp. 155–156, by W.F. Ogburn and S.C. Gilfillan, published in *Recent Social Trends in the United States: A Series of Monographs Prepared Under the Direction of the President's Research Committee on Social Trends,* New York: McGraw-Hill, 1933.

Radio wasn't exactly new, but it wasn't exactly old, either. The first political convention had been broadcast in 1920, and 1936 would be the first year that the radio would play a significant role in a national presidential election. During the 1930s and 1940s, as the Great Depression and World War II threatened the national economy and national security, President Franklin D. Roosevelt made use of the radio as no president had before, broadcasting 30 live "Fireside Chats" between 1933 and 1944. In 1981, President Ronald Reagan expanded this policy further through his weekly Saturday radio addresses, a habit carried over in subsequent administrations. In 2009, President Barack Obama made the weekly Saturday address an online, multimedia experience—with audio on the radio and streaming video on YouTube.

Television

In the terminology of the pre-industrial era, we are all mystics, and video and audio are our visions and locutions. We can all accurately see, and hear, things that aren't here with us. The activism possibilities of any medium that expands our experience of the world are as unlimited as the experiences themselves.

This has created both opportunities and problems. Before literacy, radio, and television, it was possible to judge a person by reputation alone. Before radio and television, it was possible to judge persons by their ideas. Before television, it was possible to judge persons by their voices. But with the advent of television, our popular culture has arguably become more visual, and in that respect also more superficial and glamour-conscious. The visual image of a face or a logo or an event, increasingly democratized with every new advancement in video technology (see Figure 10.3), has become identity itself.

Figure 10.3
The woman on the right isn't really in the room, but new three-dimensional videoconferencing technology allows employees to sit around the same table even when they're thousands of miles away. Photo: © 2008 Enrique Dans. Licensed under Creative Commons Attribution License 2.0 Generic.

The first presidential race in which television advertising was used on a significant scale was the 1952 race between Republican nominee Dwight D. Eisenhower and Democratic nominee Adlai Stevenson, but it played a far more significant role in the 1960 election between Democratic nominee John F. Kennedy and Republican nominee Richard Nixon, which featured the first live televised presidential debate. As Kennedy biographer Michael O'Brien writes:

The day before the event Kennedy looked over the set design and shooting angles; Nixon received the same invitation but declined, rejecting an opportunity to inspect the television venue.

CBS offered Nixon the services of its professional makeup artist, but Nixon refused. Instead, he had a nonexpert adviser apply a pancake makeup designed to conceal his stubble of beard. Kennedy, looking fit and tanned, needed only a small amount of makeup. Kennedy's dark blue suit provided a crisp contrast with the bleak gray background. By comparison, Nixon's light gray suit blended blandly with the set ...

The one question on everyone's lips was why did Nixon look so haggard, so worn, so grim? His facial muscles tensed, sweat appeared on his brow and cheeks; sometimes he forced a smile unrelated to his words. His eyes shifted and darted. By contrast Kennedy appeared fresh, vibrant, and relaxed.

> > > **NOTE**

See *John F. Kennedy: A Biography*, by Michael O'Brien , New York: St. Martin's Press, 2005, p. 480.

Many thousands of words have been written about the first Kennedy-Nixon debate, but very few of those words have to do with anything that Kennedy or Nixon actually said or with the content of the latter two debates (which had a smaller television audience and a less stark contrast between the candidates' telegenicity). The story that has endured is the story of how Nixon fumbled the new medium of television, whereas Kennedy conquered it.

And while no presidential debates were televised again until 1976, image has mattered more since then than before. The only two presidents of the past three decades who were *not* noted for their telegenic qualities—Jimmy Carter and George H.W. Bush—were also the only one-termers. No presidential candidate of the modern era has ever defeated an opponent who was perceived as holding a significant advantage in telegenicity or in being media savvy. Image has never lost.

But the Internet may change that. Television has many gatekeepers—the faces we most often see on it are those of the attractive actors and anchors that casting agents and media consultants have deemed most appealing. The Internet has no such gatekeepers, and the faces we see on Facebook represent a broader spectrum of humanity than the faces we see on television. The time may come when we've grown accustomed to that level of diversity and expect to see it from the television medium.

Four Online Activism Technologies That Are Still Catching On

This book focuses primarily on Internet activism technologies that have already been fully exploited in an activism context, but others are still earning their wings.

Collaborative Documents

Google Inc. has been spearheading a movement in the direction of writing collaborative documents online asynchronously through Google Docs (http://docs.google.com) and in real-time using the new, beta Google Wave service (http://wave.google.com). The activism implications of this sort of thing have not yet been fully realized, partly because the technology behind real-time multiuser document updating is still in its relative infancy, but we're one "killer app" away from contributing to talking points on-the-fly from our cell phone while standing in the line at the grocery store.

But as we speak, collaborative documents do serve some practical activism purposes. I use Google Docs when transcribing minutes from activism-related meetings, as it allows me to access them from multiple computers without having to copy them over. And Google Wave has been a boon for many activists in search of a free web teleconferencing aide.

Mobile Access

Okay, I know you can access the Internet from most cell phones these days. But right now it's horribly inconvenient to do two-thirds of the stuff I described in this book on even a high-end smartphone because of hardware and software limitations—and the high-end smartphones are out of most end-users' budgets. Over the next five years, it's very likely that smartphones will catch up to the point where they're almost as Internet-ready as laptops. When that happens, and if these new smartphones get cheap enough for mass user adoption, it will remove the artificial barrier between the activism we do "at home" and the activism we do "on site."

The iPhone has already been helpful in this regard. Apple's iPhone can run tens of thousands of applications, many of them helpful in an activism context.

> > > **NOTE**

Australian activist and blogger Alex Schlotzer has highlighted 7 iPhone apps that he considers particularly useful for activism purposes. Check his list out here: http://alexschlotzer.wordpress.com/2010/02/12/7-iphone-apps-for-activists/.

Integration of Web 2.0 Proprietary Standards

So you've got a MySpace profile, a Facebook profile, a YouTube profile, a Flickr profile, email accounts, a Twitter profile—and every time there's a new Web 2.0 application, you have to reintroduce yourself from scratch. Old profiles get dusty, passwords get lost, and things just generally get complicated. There's no permanent sense of identity; I'm Tom Head on Facebook, but someone else could become Tom Head on Friendster. The more networks there are, the greater the potential for confusion and mischief. Will this ever change? Probably, but nobody knows exactly how. Various solutions have been suggested, from shared user databases to new markup languages that integrate social identity, but the more useful ones are a threat to privacy, and the more secure ones are too useless to bother implementing. There's something here that still needs to be invented.

Security

Then there's the issue of keeping data secure. Hacking isn't as much of a problem as it used to be, to say the least, but it's still a problem—and every time a friend or colleague's account gets hacked, our ability to trust the Internet as a medium is diminished a little bit.

Your E-Activism Toolkit: Putting It All Together

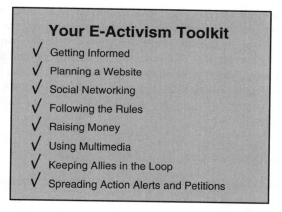

Your E-Activism Toolkit

√ Getting Informed

√ Planning a Website

√ Social Networking

√ Following the Rules

√ Raising Money

√ Using Multimedia

√ Keeping Allies in the Loop

√ Spreading Action Alerts and Petitions

So together we've walked through all of the basic Internet technologies an activist might need. Where do we go from here?

Well, that depends on who you are. I would argue that most volunteer online activists can be described as Concerned Citizens, Professional Online Activists, or Outreachers. If you fall into one of these categories, I'd offer specialized advice to keep in mind as you look over your toolkit:

Concerned Citizen

An advocacy-focused, independent/nonaffiliated online activist who often works alone. Does not usually organize actions but may promote actions organized by others. Nearly always a blogger and/or podcaster.

- **Getting Informed**—Anyone who is advocacy-focused *must* stay informed because it's impossible to advocate ideas in a context you're unfamiliar with. Stay up to date on news pertaining to your cause and, when possible, be timely in the way you engage it.

- **Building a Website**—It's usually a bad idea to make your website too personal, a mistake that some less experienced Concerned Citizens make, but there's nothing wrong with a certain amount of self-promotion. That makes it easier to cope without the social support network that an organization provides.

- **Social Networking**—Still pretty useful as a way to promote your writing and build a social network.

- **Following the Rules**—The biggest mistake Concerned Citizens tend to make is that they get caught up in drama surrounding things they've said or been called out on. It makes sense to respond to your critics if you think they're making a legitimate claim, but defending yourself can distract you from your usual efforts at advocacy. In general, don't make it too much about you; odds are good nobody wants to read that, and it's likely to make the process less enjoyable for you as well.

- **Raising Money**—Concerned Citizens have extremely low overhead. You can get free blog hosting on a server like Blogspot (www.blogspot.com), and if you get your own domain, that's still pretty cheap. However, I recommend using ad banners if you're not affiliated with a nonprofit; that'll take the edge off hosting fees and other site-related expenses and may (if you're really, really lucky) let you quit your day job and focus on your activism full-time (in which case I guess you technically wouldn't be a volunteer anymore, but it's no worse than taking a salary from a nonprofit—and there are certainly worse ways to make a living).

- **Using Multimedia**—Lots of Concerned Citizens integrate photos and video into their sites, and most podcasters are Concerned Citizens as well.

- **Keeping Allies in the Loop**—Blogging may already be what you do, and Twitter is also generally regarded as a useful tool.

- **Action Alerts and Petitions**—Link to. Or create. It's easy to create online action alerts (see Chapter 9), and not enough bloggers and podcasters do it.

Professional Online Activists

Staff members hired to set up online initiatives, either as their primary job responsibility or as a secondary responsibility, can have their work cut out for them. Different organizations have different needs and priorities, and close consultation with other staff is a must.

- **Getting Informed**—If an Online Activism Professional feels more at home with online media in general than other staff do, it's a good idea to relay relevant online news stories or other useful online content to other staff members.

- **Building a Website**—This seems to be the most common job responsibility associated with online activism—and if it's the only thing the organization really wants you to do, it might not be a good idea to argue with that.

- **Social Networking**—Social media has long replaced Google and individual organizational websites as the primary point of contact between organizations and supporters and should no longer be considered an optional part of an organization's online activism strategy.

- **Following the Rules**—The canon of professional nonprofit ethics is beyond the scope of this book, but one tension that many staffers who deal in online activism have to live with is the tension between loyalty to the organizational chain of command and commitment to an ethical online activism strategy. For most Professional Online Activists, the two inevitably come into conflict at some point or another.

- **Raising Money**—Professional Online Activists tend to have more time and money to work with than their volunteer counterparts, but it can still pay to do some things on a shoestring budget. Some of the best online options also happen to be free or cheap options.

- **Using Multimedia**—If you distribute enough content from events online, you may start feeling like a reporter before long—covering your beat, that is the organization's activity, for your online audience.

- **Keeping Allies in the Loop**—This tends to be the most neglected part of a staff online activist's work, but it's essential to building a volunteer base.

- **Action Alerts and Petitions**—Well-written action alerts are generally a *great* idea, but be sure to coordinate your message with staff who generate talking points for other media.

Outreacher

A volunteer tasked with setting up an online presence for an activist organization or political campaign—usually a small organization, or they'd hire staff to do it (see Figure 10.4).

- **Getting Informed**—Whereas Concerned Citizens build their advocacy from the ground up, Outreachers are usually well-served to collaborate with other volunteers (or, where relevant, with staff) to make sure the online message matches the rest of the organization's goals. For this reason, Outreachers don't necessarily need to stay as informed as activists who specialize in other areas, though it never hurts.

- **Building a Website**—If I've guessed right, this is the main thing you've been asked to do. I've been in your shoes, my friend. Chapter 3 is written primarily with you in mind; have at it.

- **Social Networking**—It's a good idea to set up a Facebook Fan Page for the organization and maybe a MySpace page as well. That gives you your own online supporter database that you can use to promote links, news, and events (see Figure 10.4).

- **Following the Rules**—It's especially important to maintain boundaries. Officers and staff may have *no* idea how much work is involved in what you do and can drive you into the ground with stuff that they think would take only a few minutes for you to do. Techies and treasurers are the two types of volunteers, in my experience, who are most likely to be overworked.

- **Raising Money**—If it's a small organization, it's generally best to choose options with minimal overhead. Also, make a budget up-front and make sure you're compensated on all expenses, unless you've agreed to cover some of them yourself as a donation to the organization (and this is usually a bad idea).

- **Using Multimedia**—Putting up photos of events can be a *great* way to promote a small organization because it puts a human face on things.

- **Keeping Allies in the Loop**—Outreachers are often asked to write blogs for organizations that don't really need blogs.

- **Action Alerts and Petitions**—Well-written action alerts are generally a *great* idea in any context.

Figure 10.4
This civil rights rally in Cleveland, Ohio, like many others throughout the country, was organized largely online. Photo: © 2007 Meredithwz via Flickr. Licensed under Creative Commons Attribution-ShareAlike License 2.0 Generic.

And whatever you do, take my suggestions in this book—all of them—as suggestions. Online activism is a developing field, and everybody who invests serious time into it is a pioneer, an explorer.

Today's online activism experts are experts in much the same way that fifteenth-century European cartographers were experts on the geography of the seas; most of them had a general sense of where their favorite shorelines were, more or less, but there was still plenty of unexplored territory and plenty of guesstimating going on. The best online activists are still being creative, still taking risks, and still trying to figure out what works.

Go and do likewise.

The 10 Common Online Activism Mistakes and How to Fix Them

The Internet is all about distractions. Most websites that receive financial support do so on the basis of banner advertisements that are specifically designed to persuade people to click on sites they originally had no interest in visiting. Spammers invade email inboxes with desperate offers for porn, herbal supplements, diploma mill degrees, cheap luxury watches, and anything else readers might possibly want. If you join MySpace or Facebook to promote an activist cause, it's only a matter of time before somebody starts sending you virtual flowers or invites you to join an immersive online game. The Internet, in other words, is full of opportunities to kill time.

But these are only the most obvious time wasters. Others might actually appeal to our activist impulses—activities that accomplish very little, if anything, but appeal to our goals as activists and draw huge amounts of our time away from more productive pursuits. Most of them are harmless, and some of them are fun, but none of them should be the centerpiece of an online activism strategy because they're just not very effective, pound for pound.

If you enjoy these activities and want to make them part of your official activism efforts, a few simple tweaks can change them from time wasters to productive online strategies.

1. Forwarding Unsourced Chain Letters

You've all seen the chain letters about the kid with a terminal disease whose only wish is that a message reach as many people as possible because Bill Gates has promised to give him a dollar for each copy forwarded. This would be a reasonable sort of small-scale online activism if it actually worked, but because some joker just made it up, it isn't going to help anybody. Most chain letters fall into this category, and it's always a bad idea to forward along junk. Verify a chain letter's facts before you pass it along. If you have time to click Forward, you have time to Google to see if the chain letter has already been debunked.

SORTING THE WHEAT FROM THE CHAFF

Want to know if a chain letter is legitimate? Go to www.snopes.com or urbanlegends.about.com and find out!

But sometimes chain letters are based on reality—and more often than not, they're *still* a bad idea. Take the 1998 Afghan women's rights chain letter, for example, which complained about the horrific oppression of women under the Taliban and asked readers to add their names to a petition list and forward a copy to an email address provided in the text of the letter. The trouble was that the email address wasn't functional, and because each person had a different copy of the petition, there was no realistic way to find out how many people had actually signed the thing by the time it made the rounds.

However, in some situations chain letters *can* potentially be useful—where they have called attention to some civil rights controversies that might have otherwise been overlooked, for instance. So when, if ever, is it useful to create a chain letter?

I'd say the best email chain letters are always accurate, prominently feature working website URLs (which people can visit for more information and to get involved in activism), and *do not* ask participants to add their names to a petition at the bottom. Even then, chain letters might be annoying—but at least they'll serve a purpose and might even help get the message out.

2. Getting Stuck in Blogosphere Flamewars

Here's a dirty little secret: The blogosphere, by and large, is for nonactivists. Oh, sure, some bloggers do activism. But for every prolific blogger who is out there trying to change the world, there are 10 or 20 prolific bloggers whose interest in a given issue is pretty much limited to the hypothetical. For the most part, the people who fall into the latter category tend to enjoy starting drama with each other because it's fun, because it feels vaguely important, and because it provides a cheap, low-risk substitute to the sort of adrenaline rush you get from marching with a picket sign or handing out flyers at a busy event.

Getting involved in blogosphere flamewars is fine if that's really how you want to spend your time. But if you want to get actual activism done, that isn't the way. Some blogosphere controversies can introduce you to issues you weren't familiar with before or make you rightly wary of a given organization or public figure, but most of them are wasteful and serve no purpose. Nobody ever actually *wins* a flamewar, and they make everybody involved look stupid.

If you find that visiting a blog always makes you want to post a rebuttal, it's usually best to just stop reading that blog. And if you find that visiting a blog always makes you want to defend the blogger from people posting rebuttals, it's usually best to read the blog and skip the comments field. Bloggers can always delete hurtful comments; they don't need you to stand up for them. If you must say something, send a kind, private email or post an entry—one entry, that's enough—on your own blog if you have one.

3. Participating in Unproductive Online Debate-Oriented Issue Groups

A good argument can help you refine your thinking on an issue, but good arguments are hard to come by on the Internet because in public arguments, people are generally more concerned with saving face than they are with getting to the bottom of anything.

However, if you find an especially interesting online debate group, it might be a good place to occasionally test out your talking points. Just don't spend any more time there than you have to (unless you really, really enjoy arguing with random strangers on the Internet, in which case you're in good company) .

4. Reading (or Writing) Vitriolic Garbage

Some blogs, even blogs written by people who basically agree with you on policy issues, are glorified hate sites. If you find that reading a blog or other website always makes you *angry* but doesn't really give you a productive place to channel that anger, you're probably better off not reading it.

There's definitely a place for anger in activism, and there's a role for people who are good at stirring up anger. But anger should always be directed toward a purpose. Malcolm X made people angry, for example, but he also made sure people had a steady supply of productive outlets for that anger. He didn't just get people riled up and then leave them to stew in their own juices. Anger is a good motivator for justice, but it is not a substitute for justice. It is a good means to an end, but it is not a worthwhile end unto itself. Don't be afraid to make people angry if you think it'll help your cause—but don't stir up anger for its own sake. That just contributes to burnout.

The Internet is great for distributing words and media, great for stirring up emotions, great for spreading the word about injustice. But it takes a little more work, and a lot more planning, to do something constructive with all that outrage. Most people who write online rarely, if ever, make a serious effort to connect emotional response and action. As an activist who works in online media, you have the opportunity to channel all of that passion into a real, organized movement.

5. Interpersonal Drama

Interpersonal politics are, sadly, an unavoidable part of activism. Stay involved long enough and you'll see even good people try to stab each other in the back in petty ways that are destructive to the movement, and let's not even get started on what the people who *aren't* so good might be up to.

Online media provides especially insidious opportunities for this. Offline, standing on the table at a major event and explaining in great detail and with great vitriol why you don't like another local activist would be rude and bizarre; it might even get you arrested on public disorder charges. But online, you can easily distribute the same message to 100 times as many people with less effort, less risk, and (arguably) more credibility. Online media gives us all a printing press of sorts, and it's hard to resist the opportunity to use it to right perceived wrongs in your social life, even the part of your social life that overlaps with activism.

This is a bad idea. At times, you have to back up a friend or correct a serious injustice. But when people just plain don't like each other, you're better off ignoring the situation, keeping your head down, and working on real activist goals.

6. Allowing Yourself to Be Monopolized by Attention-Starved Online Chat Users

Online chat clients are fantastic, but they have one drawback: A lot of people who are bored or lonely demand your attention every time you load the chat client up, whether you have time to give it to them or not. You don't want to be *rude* to these people because you're a nice person and because sometimes they're your friends or allies, but you don't have time to just sit there and come up with something to say every time they send you a message reading "Hello :)."

Solution? Tell these users, in a friendly way, that you're not always looking at your chat client when it's loaded and might not be able to respond to every message you receive. Then ignore them except when you actually want to talk. If the problem persists, or if you just don't want to have to deal with all that, most online chat servers also allow you to go "invisible" or list yourself as offline.

7. Installing Too Many Useless Social Networking Apps

I love Facebook—but right now, I've got 934 outstanding application requests from people who want to throw virtual livestock at me, offer me a virtual beer, or send me virtual goldfish. I can get this number down to zero by clicking Block This Application every time I reject an application request for an application I have no intention of installing.

But installing a few applications can break up the monotony and give people another way to get to know you. Personally, I enjoy a game of the online word game Lexulous as much as almost anybody—and when somebody else enjoys it, too, that tells me something about his or her interests.

8. Excessive Self-Promotion

There's a local activist—I won't say who (see mistake #5)—who organizes events under his own name rather than under the umbrella of an activist organization. He makes sure he always gets the credit for what he does (and for some things he doesn't do); he organizes some events that seem specifically designed to get his name in the papers; and every now and then he makes a long-shot bid for public office.

Don't be that guy. Don't let other people take credit for your work if you can help it, but don't try too hard to make sure you get the credit, either. With few exceptions, normal activism doesn't make people famous. It makes the world better. If you personally want to get famous, give more speeches (or write books!)—but don't confuse that with activism. The two can overlap, but they usually don't.

9. Excessive Multitasking

As I write this, I've got iChat up (where I'm strategizing about a weekend arts event), I'm working on a promotional flyer for an upcoming fundraiser, have three or four emails in draft form dealing with various activist topics, and have been texting back and forth with another local activist about listserv software. I'm managing it okay, but it has taken me 45 minutes to write this paragraph and that's probably not peak efficiency.

If you want to get something done, it's usually best to do as I say, not as I do: Focus on one small project until you finish it and then move on. Onsite activism makes this relatively easy (what else are you going to do at a rally but, well, rally?), but online activism encourages you to do too many things at once and then wonder why you haven't finished anything you've started. Prioritizing can fix that.

And remember the old web designer's maxim: *Don't build what you can't maintain.* It's great that you want to create a website for a local support group, but if you don't want to be the one who maintains it for the next two years, find somebody else who can take over after the site is online. It's great that you want to maintain an organization's group profile on Facebook, but if you don't want to be the one who uses that group profile to promote events, give someone else that responsibility. Don't overcommit.

10. General Sloth and Procrastination

Ancient Taoist philosophy places emphasis on the concept of *wu-wei*, or action without tension—"doing nothing but leaving nothing undone." The Internet will be happy to help you with the first part, but not so much the second. So how can you avoid constantly missing deadlines?

- First, set realistic goals. I seem to constantly run across people who are beating themselves up for not getting things done on time—when the reason they're not getting things done on time is because they've given themselves too much to (reasonably) do. As I noted in the previous tip, don't overcommit. Don't give yourself so much to do that you burn out. You don't need to be sacrificed to the movement (at least not yet).

- Second, watch the clock. Just as weighing often seems to have a subtle effect on people's eating and exercise habits, looking at the clock can often have a subtle, positive effect on how we spend our time.

- Third, keep a calendar. It's very hard to figure out what you have time to do if you can't remember what your existing commitments are, and the more you get involved in activism (traditional or online), the more likely you are to double- or triple-book yourself.

- Fourth, leave some flex time in your schedule. You're going to need time to relax with friends and family, endure a stomach virus, or read a few books. (I don't recommend combining the three; that can get awkward.) And in a pinch, you can use that flex time to catch up on an activist project that has been slipping away from you.

Online Activism Careers and Volunteer Opportunities

It's a basic maxim of this book that online activism is a tool you can use alongside traditional forms of activism, not a tool you can use to replace them. No matter how good the technology gets, there will always be a place and a need for more traditional activism methods.

But what if online activism is all you have? What if you're out there wandering in the social desert the Internet can sometimes become, with no local activism contacts and no sense that your work is actually going anywhere real, tangible, and human? Even if you want to specialize in online activism (and goodness knows there's a need), there's no sense in depriving yourself of local activist contacts—and opportunities, perhaps, to get paid for some things you'd do for free anyway.

Breaking In, Standing Out

Activism work isn't that much different from work in other careers. The same basic principles apply, and one of those principles is self-promotion; you have to look out for yourself. Not at the *expense* of the movement, of course, but certainly in a way that makes you look like you will become a useful part of it.

Get Yourself Connected

At the end of this appendix, I've attached a list of sites where you can find activism jobs online (see Figure B.1). These are useful whether you network—and some positions get listed on these sites but don't get much word-of-mouth attention (particularly if they represent efforts by national nonprofits to expand into new cities)—but activism work is usually about people skills and finding activism work no less so.

Figure B.1
Attending activism-related events, like the Kentucky Nonprofit Workshop on Web 2.0 shown here, can be a great way to find jobs and volunteer opportunities. It can also be more fun than it has any right to be. Photo: © 2007 Beth Kanter. Licensed under Creative Commons Attribution License 2.0 Generic.

For me, the three basic rules of networking in an activism context are to **be seen**, **be heard**, and **be nice**.

- **Being seen**—"Eighty percent of success," Woody Allen once said, "is just showing up." I doubt he had activism in mind when he said this, but he may as well have. If you already know which area of activism you're interested in specializing, keep an eye out for meetings and events sponsored by organizations that work in that area and culti-vate the habit of attending these meetings and events when you can. If this feels like too much work, okay, but ask yourself: If the idea of just showing up at events like the workshop shown in Figure B.1 doesn't sound like fun, even if I don't have to do any-thing, would I really want to make professional or volunteer commitments in this area anyway?

- **Being heard**—Stick your neck out. If you already know you want to work in a specific area of activism, you may as well go on and tell people; that way, they might think of you when they see a new job opening or a new need for volunteers. If you're enthusiastic, don't be afraid to show enthusiasm. Most activists like to see that.

- **Being nice**—Conventional wisdom says that a lot of people *buy* seats on nonprofit boards outright by making large donations to the organization, but for most organizations— most good organizations, anyway—that's a little simplistic. It would be more accurate to say that donating money to an organization shows that you are (literally) invested in the cause, but a cheaper (and less frequently anonymous) way to achieve the same objective is just to make sure you're pleasant to be around and make yourself useful as much as possible.

Look at the photo in Figure B.2, an anti-violence press conference at New Orleans City Hall at which murder victims' names were read. Everything in this picture—the banner, table, t-shirts, audio equipment, the people, even the photograph itself—came from *somewhere*. It was either given freely or purchased with donations that were given freely. Generosity—in time, money, effort, and social capital—is the lifeblood of activism.

Figure B.2

A City Hall event sponsored by Silence Is Violence, a New Orleans anti-violence group. Photo: © 2008 Bart Everson. Licensed under Creative Commons Attribution License 2.0 Generic.

Degrees of Separation

If you'd like to earn an online degree in an activism-related field, check out Appendix E, "A Directory of Online Degrees for Activists." There are programs in almost every conceivable field, at almost any conceivable price level.

But don't get too hung up on academic activism-related credentials; unless you're targeting a professional field that requires specialized training (social work, law, medicine/nursing, licensed counseling, and so on), most activism jobs don't require them. It's not uncommon to see positions that require only a high school diploma that pay more than comparable positions that require a master's degree.

The important thing is to get moving doing whatever it is that you're going to do—earning a degree, applying for positions, volunteering, or whatever it is that you're setting out to do. The most effective activists, in my experience, see it as a vocation; they see it as something they want to be part of and live into, something that defines them. It is similar, in many respects, to other sorts of jobs that have traditionally been referred to as "vocations"—public service, the military (as shown in Figure B.3), ordained ministry.

Figure B.2
A military recruiter speaks to a potential enlister at the 2009 Eastern Washington University jobs fair. Whatever your views on the military are, few lines of work have been better defined in the public consciousness as vocations. Photo: © 2009 Eastern Washington University. Licensed under Creative Commons Attribution License 2.0 Generic.

Online Nonprofit Search Databases

The best way to get started doing activism is to look at the issues that matter most to you, look for national organizations that represent those issues, and then look to see if there is a local chapter of one of these organizations. Those local chapters invariably need volunteers, and sometimes they need paid staff.

But sometimes a new organization or an organization that has been around a while but has kept a low profile will start a new initiative in your area. And sometimes the only way to find those job and volunteer opportunities is by using a national database.

Getting Your Job Search Started

As a general rule, you can find activism jobs the same way you find any other kinds of jobs: Go to general job search engines—www.monster.com is the largest—and specify that you're looking for work in the nonprofit sector; then whittle it down from there.

Idealist.org

www.idealist.org

Idealist is the largest activism-specific social network out there, and it's a great place to find social contacts, job and volunteer opportunities, events, and speakers. If you're looking for an activism job, a volunteer opportunity, or just an excuse to network with local activists, this is a great place to start.

Nonprofit Oyster

www.nonprofitoyster.com

If you're looking for a paid activism job, this large database of nonprofit-sector job opportunities can be a very useful resource.

Opportunity Knocks

www.opportunityknocks.org

Opportunity Knocks, a competitor to Nonprofit Oyster, has a jobs database of comparable size as well as useful resources on how to get started in the nonprofit sector.

Feminist Career Center

www.feminist.org/911/jobs/joblisting.asp

This job database operated by the Feminist Majority Foundation isn't as large as some of the other online job databases, but it's feminism-specific and updated often.

A Short History of Online Activism Technologies

"New technological environments are commonly cast in the molds of the preceding technology out of the sheer unawareness of their designers."

—Marshall McLuhan

The story of online activism is as old as the story of human history. The technology we think of as "online" technology is, in reality, a mix of other media more traditional to the human experience—visual media, sound, and the written word, conveyed at an appropriate and convenient speed to its audience and co-creators.

This is the story of how those technologies gradually developed into the beautiful crescendo of instant communication, inexhaustible data, bright colors, and digitized sounds that we have available to us today—technologies that, for 99.9% of human history, would have been regarded as tantamount to life in the Kingdom of Heaven.

ca. 31,000 BCE: Oldest Extant Cave Paintings

The most basic component of media technology is the need to bring an idea, a concept, an image, a phrase—an atom of media—out of the intangible, temporary space of our minds and into the real world where others can see it.

Judging by prehistoric cave paintings, such as those found in the Chauvet Cave of southern France, the need to do this is fairly basic to our species and is not contingent on civilization (that is, the development of organized social structures).

So if we begin with a human being, there is already a message to communicate. There is already a kind of advocacy. Bring that human being into an organized social context, and community organizing is inevitable.

ca. 2350 BCE: Praise Poem of Urukagina Shows Fruits of Activism

Urukagina was governor of Lagash, a province in southeastern Mesopotamia, sometime during the 24th century BCE. After his reign, a praise poem was written about him that suggests that he listened—and responded—to what we would now describe as a community organizing campaign:

> Since time immemorial, since life began, in those days, the head boatman appropriated boats, the livestock official appropriated asses, the livestock official appropriated sheep, and the fisheries inspector appropriated... The shepherds of wool sheep paid a duty in silver on account of white sheep, and the surveyor, chief lamentation-singer, supervisor, brewer and foremen paid a duty in silver on account of young lambs... These were the conventions of former times! ...

> The... administrators no longer plunder the orchards of the poor. When a high quality ass is born to a shublugal, and his foreman says to him, "I want to buy it from you"; whether he lets him buy it from him and says to him "Pay me the price I want!" or whether he does not let him buy it from him, the foreman must not strike at him in anger.

> When the house of an aristocrat adjoins the house of a shublugal, and the aristocrat says to him, "I want to buy it from you"; whether he lets him buy it from him, having said to him, "Pay me the price I want! My house is a large container—fill it with barley for me!" or whether he does not let him buy it from him, that aristocrat must not strike at him in anger...

Urukagina solemnly promised Ningirsu that he would never subjugate the waif and the widow to the powerful.

> > > **NOTE**

Learn more at "Praise of Urukagina," http://www.humanistictexts.org/sumer.htm#4%20Praise%20of%20Urukagina. Last accessed May 13, 2010.

The poem praises Urukagina's wise leadership. But in a subtle way, it also praises activism; someone had to tell him that these things took place on a widespread basis, and that suggests that a community response of some kind brought these matters to the wise governor's attention.

The praise poem itself is also a subtle work of policy advocacy—reminding any future readers that the public was well aware of how badly things had been managed before Urukagina's reforms and would notice a relapse. And while ancient Lagash was no democracy, there has never been an administration in the history of the world that could afford to be completely unaccountable to its constituents.

ca. 1157 BCE: The Medinet Habu Artisans' Strike

The first planned action for which we have specific historical evidence was an artisans' strike that took place in the mid-12th century BCE. A group of artisans, dissatisfied with poor working conditions (see Figure C.1), organized a sit-in until management—in this case, royal architects from the court of Pharaoh Rameses III—caved in and gave he workers what they demanded.

Figure C.1
In this ancient Egyptian sculpture, artisans carry tools essential to their trade. Photo: © 2006 Xuan Rosemaninovich. Licensed under Creative Commons Attribution License 2.0 Generic.

Today, more than 3,000 years later, that strategy still works.

ca. 586 BCE: Babylonian Captivity and Preservation of Jewish Scriptures

When the conquering empire of ancient Babylon forced the Jewish priestly class into exile, their objective was, in large part, to destroy Judaism so that the Jewish people could be more easily assimilated. It wasn't the first time a ruling empire tried to destroy Judaism, and it wouldn't be the last, but according to historians it did force priests to write down their stories, laws, and traditions so that they could be preserved—creating the nucleus of what we now call the Tanakh, Hebrew Bible, or Old Testament.

Much of the Hebrew Bible was activism, whether that was its original intent. In the subsequent millennia, it has been adopted by advocates of every stripe to serve many causes, good and evil, liberating and oppressive. It remains a potent source of inspiration for activists to this day.

ca. 260 BCE: Major Edicts of Ashoka

Every culture has had its own version of mass media. In the ancient world, monuments were the most effective form of mass media because they were, by an overwhelming margin, the most visible. This meant that mass media was limited primarily to those with authority to commission monuments—rulers, in other words.

During the 3rd century BCE, the Indian emperor Ashoka ordered the inscription of Buddhist precepts, social policies, and other matters of importance on massive pillars (see Figure C.2) and walls spread throughout the region. He had text that he wanted to see displayed as widely as possible, and it was the closest thing he had to a printing press or a World Wide Web.

Figure C.2
An ancient pillar displaying edicts of the Emperor Ashoka. Photo: © 2009 Varun Shiv Kapur. Licensed under Creative Commons Attribution License 2.0 Generic.

ca. 130 BCE: The Antikythera Mechanism

This mysterious device (see Figure C.3) discovered by Mediterranean divers in 1902 sounds like something out of an Indiana Jones movie: an ancient computer of unknown origin, lying discarded for more than two millennia among shipwreck debris.

But the Antikythera mechanism was not the only computer of the ancient world. Gear-driven machines—called astrolabes—were used to calculate dates of astrological importance, which could be useful to plan crop cycles, holidays, and horoscopes. What makes the Antikythera mechanism unique is that it doesn't look like any other astrolabe we've found from the period—it's incredibly complex, purportedly able to convert Egyptian and Greek calendars, predict the positions of the Moon, major stars, and five planets, and even predict eclipses.

Figure C.3
The largest fragment of the Antikythera mechanism, currently housed at the National Archaeological Museum in Athens, Greece. Photo: © 2005 Marsyas (via Wikipedia and Wikimedia Commons). Licensed under Creative Commons Attribution License 2.5 Generic.

The Antikythera mechanism was, as far as we know, a one-of-its-kind artifact—and not intended in any meaningful way for use in an activism context. But it brought the ancient world closer to the computer age than it would be for 1,500 years, as Western civilization grew increasingly focused on war, religious oppression, and addressing the realities of disease and food scarcity.

ca. AD 52: St. Paul's Epistle to the Thessalonians

The oldest part of the Christian New Testament was an epistle—an encyclical letter written by St. Paul of Tarsus to the congregation he helped create in the Greek port city of Thessalonica. In a literary and documentary sense, this letter founded Christianity.

What makes it relevant to our discussion, though, is just how it did that. Encyclical letters—letters written by leaders and distributed to be read by, and to, others—were not a particularly new concept, but under Roman persecution they were more central to the Christian faith than they had been to most other large social movements.

The Roman Empire relied primarily on monuments and visible, institutional power to serve the purposes of mass media, while the Christian church's mass media was limited to what amounted to chain letters. The success of the Christian faith in this environment, despite Roman persecution, speaks in part to the power of democratized media—a power that we are still attempting to measure.

AD 375: Talmud Bavli Commences

Rav Ashi was the first real editor of the Babylonian Talmud, and his election to lead the rabbinic academy in Sura in 375 AD got the process rolling.

The Talmud was an old-media Internet—a large volume of content from multiple sources in dialogue, cross-referenced and, as best is possible without web-surfing technology, hyperlinked. When you look at a page of Talmud (see Figure C.4), you're looking at something organic, driven by a community of scholars working from common sources, wrapped in an exhaustive roundtable dialectic and working over details of interpretation.

Figure C.4
A page from the Babylonian Talmud (Berakhot 2a). Public domain. Image courtesy of Wikimedia Commons.

AD 537: Hagia Sophia Completed

For most of human history, the most visible messages of mass media have been political and religious—because mass media by the way of monuments and works of art requires a substantial investment, investment requires power, and political and religious leaders have been the seats of power.

The Hagia Sophia in Istanbul (formerly Constantinople), the central architectural work of the Holy Roman Empire, became a symbol of stability. After the original temple on the site was destroyed in AD 532 following a revolt against the Emperor Justinian, the powers that be created a new masterwork to reinforce the sense that the empire was stable and representative of the Christian faith. The art that would ultimately fill it (see Figure C.5) also functioned as a statement of religious identity in a region that, from time to time, would shift between Christian and Muslim rule.

Figure C.5
The Virgin Mary and child, as depicted here an entrance to the Hagia Sophia in Istanbul, Turkey. Photo: © 2007 Georges Jansoone. Licensed under Creative Commons Attribution-ShareAlike License 3.0.

AD 830: The Medieval Islamic Internet

As the Christian West gradually came to distance itself from its Greek and Roman heritage, the duty of protecting the ancient scientific tradition that produced works such as the Antikythera mechanism fell on Muslim scientists, translators, and archivists. Were it not for Islam and its emphasis on the importance of learning and study, it is very likely that the Greco-Roman literary tradition as we know it would have been lost to history.

The House of Wisdom in Baghdad was the center of the 9th-century scholarly world, housing the Greek, Roman, and Persian canons and serving as a center of global scholarship. It would remain so until the 13th century, when it was destroyed by Mongol invaders—with countless volumes burned, lost to history forever.

The House of Wisdom and its fate highlights the two practical problems that print media had: scarcity and illiteracy. Only a small number of copies of texts could be produced, as they had to be hand-copied, and only scholars could read them. Centuries after the destruction of the House of Wisdom, the first of these two problems was finally solved.

1552: An Investigative Journalist Takes on the Conquistadors

Mass media has essentially gone through three eras: the monument era, the print era, and the multimedia era. The print era began in 1440 with the invention of the printing press, which made it possible to copy texts in bulk rather than relying on hand-copying. By 1552, print volumes were common. Most people couldn't read them, but a fairly large and geographically diverse literate aristocracy and clergy class could.

Appealing to this class was Dominican priest and missionary Bartolomé de las Casas (see Figure C.6), whose Brevísima Relación de la Destruccíon de la Indias (1552) woke Europe up to the genocide taking place in the Americas. It didn't change much—de las Casas had already tried, successfully convincing King Charles I of Spain to issue new, but ultimately unenforceable, human rights standards, and by personally intervening in many disputes—but from 1552 on, the European nobility could no longer claim ignorance of what was happening, and would continue to happen, to the people of the New World. They didn't stop killing, but at least they saw the blood on their hands.

Figure C.6
This 19th-century hagiographic sculpture by Miguel Noreña depicts Bartolomé de las Casas converting an Aztec family to Christianity. Photo: © 2009 Alejandro Linares Garcia. Licensed under Creative Commons Attribution-ShareAlike License 2.5.

That's what one well-connected clergy member with access to the press could do. As printing technology became cheaper and literacy became more widespread over the successive centuries, less influential individuals were able to change the map of the world.

1776: A Little Common Sense

"History," former president John Adams wrote in a 1819 letter, "is to ascribe the American Revolution to Tom Paine." But Thomas Paine wasn't a great general, a noble, an aristocrat, a clergy member—a person of any consequence, really. He was a crank, a weirdo, an anonymous pamphleteer, a person of no consequence—essentially an 18th-century blogger. And his words, mere words, made the United States possible. Specifically, one pamphlet (see Figure C.7) called Common Sense.

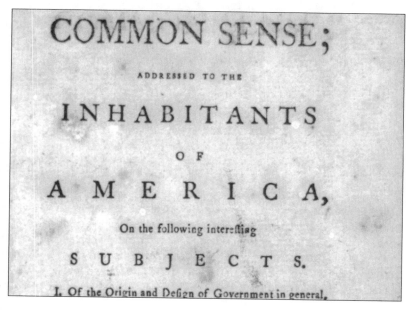

Figure C.7
The original title page of Thomas Paine's Common Sense (1776), a pamphlet that changed the world. Public domain. Image courtesy of the Library of Congress.

I'm not kidding when I call him a blogger. The thing about Common Sense is that it isn't a philosophical or historical work; it's an unapologetic work of issue advocacy, making a top-to-bottom case for revolution. It's brilliant, but it's brilliant in the way a good netroots blog is brilliant: rhetorical, pulse-racing, infuriating, written in the vernacular of the people, and taking a point of view that does not pretend to be entirely objective or even fair. And it was highly persuasive. Soon afterward, French revolutionaries, inspired by his example, would follow suit.

Today, it's unthinkable to have a revolution without a persuasive written manifesto. We owe that to Paine.

1852: Harriett Beecher Stowe, Queen of All Media

OK, so *Uncle Tom's Cabin* (1852) wasn't the first multimedia piece of advocacy ever written—the plays of Aristophanes, written to be read or performed, would probably have qualified. But the novel and the play adaptations (see Figure C.8), directly assaulted the system of agrarian slavery and, later, posed a challenge to the Jim Crow institutions of the South.

Figure C.8
Scene from a stage adaptation of Harriet Beecher Stowe's Uncle Tom Cabin *(1852). Public domain. Image courtesy of the Library of Congress.*

Just like Paine, Stowe was thanked by a president—or blamed, depending on how you look at it—for doing something much more significant, in theory, than writing a book. "So you're the little woman," President Abraham Lincoln is said to have remarked when he met her, "who started this great [American Civil] war!" But it was the play adaptations of the book, featuring a saintly but submissive hero in blackface, that made "Uncle Tom" an epithet and exposed the cruelties of racial oppression to audiences who might not have otherwise been aware of it.

1864: The Telegraph That Could Have Saved America

The electrical telegraph was the closest thing the 19th-century industrialized West had to email. Its activism applications were limited by the relative expense involved, and its potential never fully exploited for this purpose, but Halloween 1864 gave it something to do.

The presidential election of November 7, 1864, pitted incumbent President Abraham Lincoln against former general George McClellan, who ran on a subtly racist platform that called for peace with the Confederacy and subsequent preservation of Southern slavery. (McClellan's supporters also spread concerns that "miscenegation," or the intermarriage of blacks and whites, would become a problem if Lincoln won another term.) Antiwar sentiment was understandably high, given the financial and human costs of the war and its still-uncertain outcome, so it was by no means a given that Lincoln would win reelection.

He needed the eight electoral votes that the Nevada territory would have provided, if it were a state. Only one problem: There was no practical way of getting the Nevada state constitution to Congress by mail, vote on the thing, and approve it in time for it to participate in the election. Enter the telegraph. Nevada organizers wired the entire state constitution over by telegraph semi-instantly, Congress approved it, and Lincoln formally admitted Nevada to the Union—handily winning its votes.

Not that he needed them, as it turned out. But if he had, the telegraph would have changed the outcome of the American Civil War—and the course of world history.

1915: Bell Makes First Transcontinental Telephone Call

Telegraphs are all well and good, but you can't talk on them. The age of distributed audio media—radio for mass media, telephone for one-on-one media—came about in the early 20th century, and that gave instant communication a human touch it never had before.

Alexander Graham Bell (see Figure C.9) patented the telephone in 1875, and over the course of the next 40 years the infrastructure to support it was slowly built. When Bell called San Francisco from New York in 1915, it was a sign that the telephone had come into its own.

Figure C.9
Prominent inventor and advocate for the deaf Alexander Graham Bell, the first person to patent the telephone, photographed in 1922. Public domain. Image courtesy of the Library of Congress.

The telephone changed activism in so many ways that it would be nonsensical to speak of "telephone activism." It's used to organize volunteers, raise funds, get out the vote, spread information, lobby officials, field calls from affected communities—it has become essential to the way activists do business.

1946: ENIAC Completed

The first true electronic computer was the U.S. Army's Electronic Numerical Indicator and Computer (see figure C.10), commonly known as ENIAC, used to calculate long-distance ballistics and the blast radius of nuclear weapons. It took up the size of a small house, had more than five million parts, required a team of scientists equipped with punchcards to operate, and had less processing power—substantially less—than an iPod does today. But it was what it was.

Figure C.10
The Electronic Numerical Integrator and Computer (ENIAC), as originally housed at the U.S. Army's Ballistic Research Laboratory in Aberdeen, Maryland. Public domain. Image courtesy of Wikimedia Commons.

> > > **N O T E**

> ENIAC was operated primarily by women, who made up the vast majority of early computer programmers. Men would largely take over the field in the 1950s and have largely controlled the IT industry ever since—though this is slowly beginning to change as more women major in computer science.

1958: Invention of Integrated Circuit

Before Jack Kilby built the first working integrated circuit over the summer of 1958, computers were massive, much as the ENIAC was, because they relied on vacuum tubes. After Kilby's invention, they shrunk to the size where they could be more easily adapted to university and business use—and, ultimately, to personal computing.

1960: Kennedy-Nixon Debate

Until 1960, presidential candidates just didn't debate in a broadcast venue. The first televised presidential debate was also the first debate between major-party candidates ever carried over the radio (party primary debates had been broadcast as early as 1948 but never a debate between the two nominees).

1960 was a victory for participatory democracy and all forms of mass media, not just television, inasmuch as it represented voters' first opportunity to see or hear presidential candidates debate each other. Unfortunately for Richard Nixon, television voters also saw a sweaty, clammy, shifty-eyed character whose extemporaneous mannerisms were not well-suited for television viewing; he performed fine in speeches, but being television-friendly for a debate was another matter. Kennedy, on the other hand, may have been the most television-friendly presidential candidate there had ever been—he was great-looking, tanned, young, and completely calm.

Nixon would later improve, but nobody forgot how important it is to look polished on camera. And, coming from a generation largely unfamiliar with television and perhaps fearing a Nixon-esque experience, presidential nominees would not debate again on television until 1976.

1962: Bell Systems Offers IMTS, First Automatic Mobile Cell Phone System

Landline telephones can be really useful if you happen to be near the right one. The trouble is that if you're expecting a call at home, you have to be at home to receive it—and if you're expecting a call at work, you have to be at work to receive it. This makes telephones only marginally practical for activism, particularly for young adults and others who spend a lot of time going from place to place.

And then there's the infrastructure problem. If you live in a rural area, particularly in the developing world, it may not even be possible to get a landline.

Cell phones solve this problem by allowing people to carry telephones around with them wherever they go, sending and receiving signals by way of a large international network of cell phone towers that provide coverage to the entire industrialized world and to much of the developing world as well (see figure C.11).

Figure C.11
This cell phone charging station makes it possible for rural Ugandans to use mobile and Internet technology. Photo: © 2008 Ken Banks / kiwanja.net. Licensed under Creative Commons Attribution License 2.0 Generic.

Although they didn't catch on until the 1990s, the first cell phones became an option in 1962—and "car phones" an option for the very rich even prior to that. Humphrey Bogart's character famously uses just such a phone in *Sabrina* (1954).

1969: ARPANET Created

ARPANET, the U.S. Department of Defense project that would later morph into the Internet, originally consisted of networked computers at four universities: Stanford, UCLA, UC-Santa Barbara, and the University of Utah. By the end of 1980, the number had grown to more than 200.

1971: Project Gutenberg and the Birth of eBooks

ARPANET was first able to transfer files through FTP—File Transfer Protocol—in 1971, and a young man named Michael Hart used his computer privileges at the University of Illinois to type public domain texts in and distribute them electronically. (He called the transcribed texts "eBooks," a term that is still in use today.) By 1987, he had transcribed more than 300. By 2010, Hart and his team of volunteers had transcribed more than 30,000.

Much like the House of Wisdom in Baghdad, Project Gutenberg represents a step forward in the preservation of texts. As a practical matter, eBooks can be distributed so easily, and on such a large scale, that it is far more difficult to intentionally destroy a book—and far easier to store one. A single 2TB hard drive can archive more than 40 million books; the Library of Congress, the largest physical library on Earth, holds 31 million. As more books are made available in an electronic format by Project Gutenberg, Amazon.com, and Google Books (books.google.com), the collective wisdom of the world slowly becomes safer.

1972: Community Memory

The commercial Internet wasn't a live possibility for most people until the early 1990s, but you don't need the Internet to create electronic social networking. Leopold's Records in Berkeley, California began featuring an electronic message board and jobs/notes listing—essentially, a precursor to Craigslist (www.craigslist.com)—on a computer, dubbed Community Memory, in 1972.

It couldn't be accessed remotely, but because Leopold's Records was a cultural center among Berkeley's student community, Community Memory was a perfect instrument to demonstrate electronic media's power to share information among activists and others.

1977: The Personal Computer Takes Off

Internet activism as we know it would not be realistically possible without personal computers, but the size, expense, and difficulty associated with computers initially made them unsuitable for home use. This changed in 1977 with the Apple II, and its successors—such as the IBM PC and IBM PCjr, the Tandy 1000, and the Macintosh—would further expand the personal computer market during the 1980s.

1978: Ward Christensen Creates the First Dialup BBS

Berkeley's Community Memory project was a great idea, but in practice it wasn't that different from a traditional bulletin board; instead of walking up and tacking notes to a corkboard, you would walk up and type notes on a computer. It's not really new activism; it's old activism with slightly better technology.

Enter the dialup bulletin board system (BBS), which allowed users to call up a shared system like Community Memory using a modem (see Figure C.12), and leave messages and files for other users. Over time, BBS's became more sophisticated—often featuring large file libraries and online games. They were, in effect, slow, small, low-tech versions of Facebook.

Figure C.12
This desktop computer, an Amiga 3000UX, hosted a two-line BBS in 1994. Photo: © Acp via Wikipedia/Wikimedia Commons. Licensed under Creative Commons Attribution-ShareAlike License 3.0.

1984: Tom Jennings Creates FidoNet

The drawback of BBS's is that most of them were small and local. I called my BBS the Mos Eisley Cantina, named after the cantina in Star Wars, and it had maybe 100 semi-regular users in the Jackson/metropolitan area of Mississippi. But that's not exactly a vast international network.

OK, neither was FidoNet, really. But it did provide BBSs a way to link up discussion forums, private messages, and file databases by calling local "hubs" that were connected to a geographically comprehensive international network of other "hubs." Messages did not travel as quickly as they do on the Internet, relying as they did on dialup, but they made it possible for people to have conversations with larger numbers of people on a wider variety of topics. It was, in many ways, culturally similar to a smaller, slower, low-tech Internet.

1989: CompuServe Goes Online

CompuServe had already established itself as a subscription-based BBS by 1989, when it became the first major commercial Internet service provider (ISP) by offering email and Usenet services.

The launch of CompuServe's commercial Internet services marked the beginning of the Internet age, but the services available—email, Usenet, FTP, telnet—were fairly basic at first, accessed at the time through what amounted to a text-based BBS interface.

1994: The World Wide Web

Generally speaking, when we think of the Internet, we tend to think of Web sites. But until Tim Berners Lee invented the World Wide Web in 1991, there was no such animal—and until Mosaic Netscape was released in 1994, there was no way for ordinary users to access it.

Imagine an Internet with no http:// addresses, no www. domains, and it's very easy to see why the Internet was not widely used by non-students before 1994. Although Usenet veterans speak of "eternal September," the increasing number of students who began accessing the Internet in Fall 1993 and beyond, most individual users and companies didn't have any kind of Internet presence until the Web.

Although not yet successfully exploited (see Figure C.13), the Web would make it possible for presidential candidates to advocate their platform, access media, and raise money online.

Figure C.13
Until the Barack Obama and Ron Paul campaigns of 2008, Howard Dean in 2004 became the first major-party presidential candidate to make serious use of the Internet for fundraising and organizing purposes. Photo: © 2007 Steve Bott. Licensed under Creative Commons Attribution License 2.0 Generic.

2004: Facebook Is Founded

The first widely-used social networking site was Friendster, founded in 2002, which was soon supplemented by MySpace, founded in 2003. But Facebook perfected the concept. Founded as a site for Harvard students to network, sort of like a highly sophisticated online version of Berkeley's Community Memory, it soon expanded to include other universities, then companies, then metropolitan areas. As of May 2010, it boasts more than 400 million active users.

The rise of Facebook corresponded with the rise of what commenters often call Web 2.0: the use of the World Wide Web to not only distribute content through Web sites, but also to allow for more communication by and among users. Weblogs, such as DailyKos (see Figure C.14), helped put this technology to use in an activism context.

Figure C.14
Markos Moulitsas Zùniga, founder of DailyKos, speaks at a Teamsters rally in Chicago, Illinois.
Photo: © 2007 Colorado Luis. Licensed under Creative Commons Attribution License 2.0 Generic.

Glossary of Terms

action   Something specific that is being done to create a desirable outcome. Actions are the things that activists organize and participate in; they are the active, potent, realized form of activism. A protest is an action, so is a phone-in campaign to your local legislator, or a boycott, or a strike.

action alert   Also known as a call to action, an action alert is an email or other notification sent to activists and potential activists informing them of an action and asking them to participate. Online action alerts generally focus on contacting elected officials and other decisionmakers about a given problem, promoting a boycott, or signing a petition. For more about action alerts, see Chapter 9, "Action Alerts and Online Petitions."

advocacy   Activism oriented toward rationally persuading the undecided to adopt your cause, persuading supporters to take a more active role in your cause, or persuading adversaries to oppose your cause less aggressively. A **blog** can be a useful advocacy tool.

agenda   The short- to moderate-term objectives of your organization, as opposed to the more perennial, long-term objectives that tend to make up an organization's **mission statement**. An organization's agenda can change from day to day.

allies   Those who support a cause but are not necessarily **stakeholders**, for example, are not directly, personally, and immediately affected by the cause's success or failure. The feminist movement, for example, includes many progressive male allies whose rights are not directly restricted by antifeminist legislation.

AltaVista   http://www.altavista.com   Founded in 1995, AltaVista was the most popular online search engine of the pre-Google era and is still in use today. One of its more enduring features is Babel Fish (http://babelfish.altavista.com), which automatically translates text from one language into another. For more about AltaVista, see Chapter 2, "How to Research Issues and Stay Informed."

alternative media   Media that is not owned by one of the major media conglomerates (the New York Times Company, Gannett, etc.), though this distinction is being lost now that some of the alternative media conglomerates (such as Village Voice Media) are larger and more successful than some of the more traditional media conglomerates. Generally speaking, alternative media is media that tends to be locally owned, experimental, and more friendly to activism (particularly left-wing activism) than traditional media outlets. The term **independent media** is used specifically to refer to media outlets that are not owned by national media conglomerates.

AOL Instant Messenger (AIM)   http://www.aim.com   An **instant messaging (IM)** protocol that allows users to chat one-on-one in real time. For more about AIM, see Chapter 8, "How to Keep Allies and Supporters in the Loop."

AsianAve   http://www.asianave.com   One of three ethnically-focused social networking sites owned by Community Connect Inc. (the other two being **BlackPlanet** and **MiGente**), AsianAve focuses on Asian Americans as a target audience, though others are welcome as well.

augmented reality   A term coined by astrophysicist Tom Caudell to refer to the use of electronic media overlaid against the real world—the computer-generated sports scores shown at the bottom of a television screen during a football game, for example.

BBS (Bulletin board system)   A BBS is essentially a mini-Internet, usually operated by a volunteer on a single computer that individual users can connect to by dialing up with their modems. BBSs were extremely popular in the pre-Internet era, but interest in them has largely died down.

BlackPlanet   http://www.blackplanet.com   One of three ethnically-focused social networking sites owned by Community Connect Inc. (the other two being **AsianAve** and **MiGente**), BlackPlanet focuses on African Americans as a target audience, though others are welcome as well.

blog (Web log)   A website made up of updated content in journal-style reverse chronological order, usually one that allows visitors to publicly comment on individual entries. Most blogs are in effect public online diaries, but blogs can also be used to keep people updated on activism and causes. Examples of successful activism blogs include RaceWire (http://www.racewire.org) and Capital Defense Weekly (http://www.capitaldefenseweekly.com). For more about blogs, see Chapter 8.

blogger   Someone who writes or writes for a **blog**.

blogosphere   A slang term used to refer to the virtual community created when bloggers comment on and link to each others' articles. The term blogosphere is often used in the context of topic-specific blogs; for example "the feminist blogosphere" might be used to refer collectively to the most frequently-visited and frequently-linked feminist blogs.

blogroll   A list of other blogs provided on a blog site. In addition to providing visitors with additional reading material and creating **blogospheres**, this was also an early form of **social networking** because it functions as a sort of **reputation system** by implying that the blog on which the blogroll is hosted endorses, in some vague and general sense, the quality of the content on the blog sites it advertises.

Capwiz   http://capitoladvantage.com/capwiz   An online action alert system that allows for automated grassroots lobbying to legislators and other public officials. For more about Capwiz, see Chapter 9.

chain letter   An email forwarded along from person to person, in which each recipient is expected to add his or her name to a petition appended at the bottom. Some chain letters are intended to function as **action alerts**, but because of the practical impossibility of tracking the number of people who add their names to the petition, they don't function very effectively in that role. Internet users tend to find chain letters extremely annoying.

civil disobedience   Nonviolent resistance to civil authority. Examples of civil disobedience include sit-ins, union strikes, and **hacktivism**.

CMS (Content Management System)   A piece of software intended to simplify the management of website content, though most are complicated enough to use that they're not practicable for small nonprofits.

coalitioning   Building alliances between organizations with overlapping objectives. For example, the Safe Schools Coalition (http://www.safeschoolscoalition.org) is an anti-bullying/ anti-discrimination organization focusing on LGBT youth, so coalition members include LGBT rights organizations, youth centers, and suicide prevention programs, among others.

Community Memory   The first computer **BBS** (bulletin board system), operated onsite at Leopold's Records in Berkeley, California from 1973 to 1975.

community organizing   Organizing **stakeholders** and **allies** into a **grassroots** movement, usually one that schedules **actions**. Community organizing is often associated with left-wing movements, but every form of grassroots activism ultimately relies on community organizing in order to succeed.

constituency   Those to whom one is accountable. For elected officials, voters are the constituency; for staff and volunteers at activist organizations, the membership is the constituency.

copylefted   Copyrighted, but with a stated license agreement that allows for some degree of royalty-free distribution. Common licenses used for copylefted content are **Creative Commons** and GNU Public License. Some licenses allow for completely unlimited distribution, some allow for unlimited distribution as long as the content is not used for commercial purposes, some require it to be attributed, some require that it not be modified or used in derivative content, and some have other applicable terms. The most common copylefted licenses allow for unlimited redistribution with attribution, but be sure to check which terms apply to the piece of content you'd like to use. Copylefted content is not the same as **public domain** content, which is not copyrighted at all. For more about copylefted content, see Chapter 7, "How to Use Multimedia as an Activism Tool."

core beliefs   The guiding principles of an organization or movement, often summarized in a **mission statement**.

core group   The most active or high-ranking members of an organization. As an organization grows, it becomes difficult or impossible for all active members to feel like they're part of an organizational core group, which necessitates the creation of specialized committees or task forces into which resources may be channeled.

Creative Commons   http://www.creativecommons.org   A 501(c)(3) nonprofit organization dedicated to the future of **copylefted** content. Creative Commons licenses allow copyright holders to license out content for redistribution under controlled circumstances. For more about Creative Commons, see Chapter 7.

Delicious   http://www.delicious.com   A social bookmarking site in which users can tag and highlight web content to make it more visible to users interested in similar content. It was founded in 2003 and purchased in 2005 by Yahoo!. For more about Delicious, see Chapter 2.

Digg   http://www.digg.com   A social bookmarking site, similar to **Delicious**, in which users can promote web pages that they consider interesting. Founded in 2004. For more about Digg, see Chapter 2.

digital divide   The growing gap between those who have Internet access and those who don't. In the past, the term was used primarily in the United States to address access disparities between low-income, female, or minority Americans and higher-income, male, or white Americans. Now the term is often used in a global sense to refer to differing opportunities between industrialized and developing countries. In Iceland, for example, 89% of the population has Internet access, while in the Democratic Republic of the Congo, only 0.4% of the population does. The Internet being central to the global economy and global media, disparities in Internet access both reflect and reinforce other economic disparities, widening the gap between the rich and the poor. For more about the digital divide, see Chapter 1, "Online Activism 101."

direct action   Protests intended to have a direct effect on others, rather than relying entirely on persuasive speech. Strikes and sit-ins, for example, are forms of direct action because they are not merely protests in the traditional sense; they directly challenge authority.

distance learning   Education that takes place over a distance through the use of media, whether that media is print (as in the case of correspondence courses), audio, television, or the Internet. Online distance learning, as profiled in Appendix E, "A Directory of Online Degrees for Activists," has caught on in recent years.

e-activism   The use of the Internet and other, related new media (such as cell phone technology) to promote activist causes.

e-commerce   Commerce that takes place online. Internet fundraising is sometimes lumped into the same general category as e-commerce because it uses e-commerce software.

e-petition   A petition that can be filled out online, usually without a signature. It's seldom an effective way of advocating an issue because there is not usually a way to validate that all of the signatures are genuine and come from different people. For more about e-petitions, see Chapter 9.

echoes   FidoNet discussion forums. Precursors to **newsgroups**.

embedding   Including a piece of standalone content, such as streaming video or a **widget**, on a website.

Facebook   http://www.facebook.com   The world's largest and most frequently-used social networking site, with more than 300 million active users. Facebook is distinguished from other sites primarily by its streamlined interface, its emphasis on using real names rather than aliases, and features that make it easy to search for and connect with real-life contacts. It was founded in 2004. For more about Facebook, see Chapter 4, "Engage with Social Networking Sites."

FidoNet   http://www.fidonet.org   Founded in 1984, FidoNet was a precursor to the Internet that operated based on a electronic **phone tree** of **BBS** systems that distributed messages, files, and other content through an international network.

Flickr   http://www.flickr.com   The world's largest image hosting service, with more than four million user-uploaded photographs. Flickr combines the features of an online photo album with the features of an online **social networking** site and allows for easy searching based on **tags** and **Creative Commons** licenses. Founded in 2004. For more about Flickr, see Chapter 7.

Friendster   http://www.friendster.com   The first popular **social networking** site, though now dwarfed considerably by the much larger **Facebook** and **MySpace**. Founded in 2002, Friendster has about 90 million active users.

geotagging   The use of mobile phone GPS technology to intentionally communicate one's physical location to others using the Internet. For more about possible activism applications of geotagging, see Chapter 10, "It's Your World, So Change It."

Google   http://www.google.com   The most popular site on the Internet, the Google search engine is how most people locate and manage content. Google also has various subsidiaries, as discussed in Chapter 2.

grassroots   A movement that is community-driven that grows and spreads organically, rather than a movement that is planted and intentionally spread without input from the community.

grassroots lobbying   Lobbying by members of the community, rather than by professional activists.

ground rules   The fundamental rules of conduct that govern an organization. For more about ground rules, see Chapter 5, "A Short Guide to the Ethics and Etiquette of Online Activism."

hacktivism   Breaking into computers or sites, spreading viruses, and using other unconventional and/or illegal means to promote a cause. For more about hacktivism, see Chapter 5.

HTML   Hypertext Markup Language, the programming language in which web pages are written.

Hulu   http://www.hulu.com   A website operated jointly by NBC Universal, Fox, and the Walt Disney Company to allow for free, legal streaming online delivery of television programs and movies.

ICQ   A popular but somewhat outdated realtime one-on-one **instant messaging (IM)** proto-col. For more about ICQ, see Chapter 8.

Idealist.org   http://www.idealist.org   A **social networking** and job search website created specifically for activists and nonprofit organizations.

independent media   Media that is not owned by a national media conglomerate.

instant messaging (IM)   Real-time online text-based chat using Internet technologies such as **AOL Instant Messenger** or **ICQ**. Most social networking sites, including Facebook, now also incorporate optional instant messaging capabilities.

IRC   Internet Relay Chat. A popular realtime group chat protocol that also allows for one-on-one chat. For more about IRC, see Chapter 8.

LinkedIn   http://www.linkedin.com   A résumé distribution/**reputation system** site that uses a **social networking** model. LinkedIn is distinguished from other social networking sites in that it is useful primarily for business-related networking and not used very much for social interaction.

meme   A word invented by biologist Richard Dawkins to describe contagious ideas.

MiGente   http://www.migente.com   (Spanish: "my people") One of three ethnically-focused social networking sites owned by Community Connect Inc. (the other two being **AsianAve** and **BlackPlanet**), MiGente focuses on Latinos as a target audience, though others are wel-come as well.

mission statement   An organizational's statement of intent—what it is, what it is for, and what it aims to do.

MMS (Multimedia Messaging Service)   A cell phone text message protocol that allows for the sending of images and other multimedia content.

MySpace   http://www.myspace.com   The second most popular **social networking** site, second only to **Facebook**. Founded in 2003, MySpace currently has 125 million users. For more about MySpace, see Chapter 4.

news aggregator   A site that collects news on a given topic so that it can be distributed to people who are interested in that specific topic. For more about news aggregators, see Chapter 2.

newsgroups   Online discussion forums operated through an old, well-established distribu-tion network called Usenet.

Ning   http://www.ning.com   A **social networking** hosting service that allows users to cre-ate their own social networking sites. For more about Ning, see Chapter 4.

Open Directory Project   http://www.dmoz.org   An online directory of 4.6 million sites sites organized into 590,000 topic categories.

open source   Software in which the source code is distributed and available for modifica-tion. Open source code is usually **copylefted**.

Orkut   http://www.orkut.com   A **social networking** site operated by **Google**.

PayPal   http://www.paypal.com   A web-based service that allows users to purchase products and support causes online while protecting credit card information. For more about PayPal, see Chapter 6, "How to Raise Funds."

phone bank   A form of telephone activism in which volunteers or staff call people on a list, sequentially, asking for donations or other participation. Similar in practice, but not usually in intent, to telemarketing.

podcasting   Giving an audio or video presentation over the Internet, usually on a regular basis. For more about podcasting, see Chapter 7.

press advisory   A short statement describing an **action** or other event distributed to the media in advance. Distinguished from a **press release** in that it is written as a point-by-point summary, not as a narrative description. For more about press advisories, see Chapter 8.

press release   An article, usually written by an organization, in which the text itself or the substantive content is intended for redistribution through local media outlets. For more about press releases, see Chapter 8.

public domain   Material that has been released from copyright due to expiration, release of the material by the author(s), or intrinsic public domain status (material produced by the U.S. government, for example, is generally public domain). For more about public domain material, see Chapter 7.

reputation system   A system in which the credibility of an individual, group, product, or piece of web content is determined at least in large part by reputation. A good example of a reputation system is the auction site eBay (http://www.ebay.com), in which merchants are always listed alongside the ratings given to them by buyers. **Social bookmarking** sites rely explicitly on a reputation system, and **social networking** sites rely implicitly (or in the case of **LinkedIn**, clearly and directly) on it.

RSS (Really Simple Syndication)   A protocol that allows for readers of blogs and other frequently-updated content to receive automatic updates and partial or full text of relevant content as it is produced.

satyagraha   ("grasp the truth") A devotee of the nonviolent activism philosophy of Mohandas Karamchand Gandhi (1869–1948).

search engine   A website that indexes and then allows the searching of web sites or other online content on a large scale. Examples of popular search engines include **AltaVista** and **Google**.

Second Life   A **virtual world** website that allows online users to build personas and interact with the personas of others. For more on Second Life, see Chapter 7.

SEO   Search Engine Optimization. Writing web content in a manner that will allow it to be easily found by search engines.

SMS (Short Message Service)   The most common protocol used for cell phone text messages, as distinguished from **MMS** (which allows multimedia content to be sent along with messages).

social bookmarking   A site, such as **Delicious** or **Digg**, that indexes web pages highlighted by users and flagged as interesting or otherwise notable. For more about social bookmarking, see Chapter 2.

social networking   Using the Internet to connect people on a personal level. The early social networking sites were by and large Internet dating sites, but thanks to the innovations of **Friendster, MySpace**, and **Facebook**, social networking has now become something that almost everybody can benefit from—and a particularly effective tool for activists. For more on social networking, see Chapter 4.

spam   Unsolicited bulk commercial email. The Internet equivalent to telemarketing, but far more damaging to infrastructure (as spam clogs up email delivery points, taking up bandwidth that could otherwise be made available for legitimate emails).

stakeholder   Someone who has a vested personal interest in a cause and is most directly affected by it. If the cause is black civil rights, for example, stakeholders are African Americans; if the cause is gay rights, stakeholders are lesbians, bisexuals, and gay men; and so forth. Those who support a cause but are not in the category of people most directly affected by it are **allies**.

status update   Text distributed on **Facebook, Twitter**, or other **social networking** sites to show what a person or group is doing or otherwise wants to broadcast at that time. Most status updates are 140 characters or fewer, so they tend to be concise; they are also updated periodically. On Twitter, a status update is called a **tweet**.

talking points   Prepared statements or arguments that can be used to defend a specific position vis-a-vís a policy or other agenda item. For more about talking points, see Chapter 9.

tweet   A **status update** distributed using **Twitter**.

Twitter   A **social networking** site dedicated entirely to short **status updates** (called **tweets**), which can be used to keep a large number of people updated at the same time. For more on Twitter, see Chapter 8.

urban legend   A "friend of a friend" story that is distributed until it becomes widely known, regardless of its veracity or lack thereof. Not all urban legends are false, but most are.

viral video   A video that is widely distributed.

virtual world   A simulated, multi-user online world such as **Second Life**. For more on virtual worlds, see Chapter 7.

VoIP (Voice over IP)   A protocol that allows the Internet to function as a substitute for a traditional telephone or cell phone line. For more about VoIP, see Chapter 7.

volunteer   Someone who does work voluntarily without pay. Volunteers are my primary audience for this book and make up the vast majority of activists, but most of the issues that affect volunteers also affect staff.

Web 1.0   Web design that implements one-way communication of the sort you would get from a newspaper, television, or radio; they send and you receive, with minimal direct participation.

Web 2.0   Web design that implements two-way communication, allowing visitors to partici-pate in and/or contribute to site content in a meaningful way.

widget   A piece of content that can be **embedded** into a web page to provide additional functionality. For more on widgets, see Chapter 7.

Wiki   A **Web 2.0** website format that allows users to change or submit changes to content rather than relying exclusively on web designers. The best-known Wiki is **Wikipedia**. For more about **Wikis**, see Chapter 8.

WikiLeaks   http://www.wikileaks.com   A website made up of leaked documents from all over the world, allowing users—particularly those living in or interested in oppressive countries—to keep an eye on their governments.

Wikimedia Commons   http://www.wikimedia.org   A repository of **public domain** and **copylefted** content.

Wikipedia   http://www.wikipedia.org   A massive collaborative, **Web 2.0**-style online ency-clopedia operating under a **Creative Commons** license.

XML (Extensible Markup Language)   A programming language that supplements **HTML** and allows websites to operate more like other software applications.

Yahoo!   http://www.yahoo.com   An online media conglomerate that, prior to the advent of **Google**, was the largest entity on the Internet. Yahoo! is noted primarily for its directory, though that directory has now largely been replaced by the **Open Directory Project** and **Google**'s directory option. For more about Yahoo!, see Chapter 2.

YouTube   http://www.youtube.com   A Web 2.0 video-sharing website, now owned by Google, that receives more than one billion hits per day. For more about YouTube, see Chapter 7.

zap action   An activist event organized on short notice, usually with small groups, and tar-geted for maximum effect. Zap actions are often announced using **Twitter** or **SMS**.

Online Degree Programs for Activists

"Education is dangerous. It is enough if they can count up to one hundred...Every educated person is a future enemy."

—Martin Bormann, secretary to Adolf Hitler

This book deals mainly with how to use online technology to do activism itself, but another way the Internet can be put in the service of your cause is by making you a more qualified and well-rounded activist. At times, a college degree can be a significant help in this department, and some college programs are specifically tailored to fields that may prove helpful to activists.

The chapter lists bachelor's degree programs, master's degree programs, and, yes, doctorates, all of which can be completed at least mostly online, and most of which can be completed with no travel or on-campus residency.

WHERE ARE THE TWO-YEAR DEGREE PROGRAMS?

This chapter doesn't describe online A.S./A.A. associate's degree programs, such as those offered by your local community college, because they're probably already offered online by your local community college and at a cheaper rate (with in-state tuition) than anything I could list in this chapter. It's also hard to assess the degree to which an A.A./A.S. degree is activism focused when most of them tend to be fairly general, focusing on prerequisites and foundation coursework.

However, if you have miscellaneous lower-level credit that you'd like to turn into an associate's degree, all three the schools listed in the credit bank section for bachelor's programs—Charter Oak State College (www.cosc.edu), Excelsior College (www.excelsior.edu), and Thomas Edison State College (www.tesc.edu)—also offer two-year degrees, with the same level of flexibility regarding transfer credit and alternative credit sources.

Finishing Your Bachelor's Degree: Credit Bank Programs

If you already have course credits, have professional certifications that might be assessable for credit, or are really good at tests, a credit bank program is probably the fastest and least expensive way to finish your bachelor's degree.

Credit bank programs accept the following:

- Unlimited transfer credit from other regionally accredited institutions, as long as the credit is not duplicative.

- Credit by examination through CLEP, DSST, and other testing programs.

- Credit awarded through assessment of professional certifications and exams.

- In many cases, "portfolio assessment" of work experience and other documented off-campus educational experience for credit.

They also tend to be relatively inexpensive.

The three schools listed next were all created by state legislatures during the Vietnam War to allow overseas military personnel to complete their degrees off campus. Two of them (Charter Oak State College and Thomas Edison State College) are still state run; the other (Excelsior College) was state run for 26 years and then went private in 1998.

Charter Oak State College

Residency: None required.

Located in: New Britain, Connecticut

Website: www.cosc.edu

Relevant degree programs: Bachelor of Arts (B.A.) or Bachelor of Science (B.S.) in general studies, with a concentration in organizational leadership, organizational management, or political science, or an individualized concentration designed by the student with special faculty approval.

Summary: Created by the Connecticut State Legislature in 1973, COSC is probably the least expensive way for someone with old transcripts, but no degree, to finish their bachelor's degree.

Excelsior College

Residency: None required.

Located in: Albany, New York

Website: www.excelsior.edu

Relevant degree programs: Bachelor of Arts (B.A.) or Bachelor of Science (B.S.) in communication studies, with emphasis in organizational communication; B.A. or B.S. in political science.

Summary: Founded in 1971 as the Regents College program of the New York State Department of Education; went private and became Excelsior College in 2001. Excelsior is particularly well-known for its optional proprietary Excelsior College Examinations (ECEs), which students can take onsite at local testing centers throughout the country for credit.

Full disclosure: I earned my own bachelor's degree through the Regents College program in 1996.

Thomas Edison State College

Residency: None required.

Located in: Trenton, New Jersey

Website: www.tesc.edu

Relevant degree programs: Bachelor of Arts (B.A.) in environmental studies, labor studies, political science, or social sciences; Bachelor of Science (B.S.) in human services, with emphasis in community services; B.S. in organizational leadership.

Summary: Created in 1972, TESC is probably the best option for anyone who has already earned some credit and wants to finish a bachelor's degree. It's inexpensive, state run, and offers the widest range of credit assessment options of any school on this list.

Accreditation and Avoiding Diploma Mills

Every school listed in this appendix holds U.S. regional accreditation or, in the case of schools not located in the United States, an equivalent non-U.S. level of recognition. But if you look on the Internet for additional schools and additional programs, you'll encounter a minefield of shady online diploma mills. How can you tell the scams from the real educational opportunities?

When looking at schools that offer degrees online or by correspondence, it is especially important to verify the school's accreditation status. In the United States, the highest standard is *regional* accreditation—accreditation by one of the six regional agencies that inspects nearly all of America's legitimate brick-and-mortar schools, from your local public elementary school to Harvard. These six agencies are

- The Middle States Association of Colleges and Schools (www.msche.org), which covers Delaware, the District of Columbia, Maryland, New Jersey, New York, Pennsylvania, Puerto Rico, and the U.S. Virgin Islands.

- The New England Association of Schools and Colleges (www.neasc.org), which covers Connecticut, Maine, Massachusetts, New Hampshire, Rhode Island, and Vermont.

- The North Central Association of Colleges and Schools (www.ncacasi.org), which covers Arizona, Arkansas, Colorado, Illinois, Indiana, Iowa, Kansas, Michigan, Minnesota, Missouri, Nebraska, New Mexico, North Dakota, Ohio, Oklahoma, South Dakota, West Virginia, Wisconsin, and Wyoming.

- The Northwest Association of Accredited Schools (www.northwestaccreditation.org), which covers Alaska, Idaho, Montana, Nevada, Oregon, Utah, and Washington.

- The Southern Association of Colleges and Schools (www.sacscoc.org), which covers Alabama, Florida, Georgia, Kentucky, Louisiana, Mississippi, North Carolina, South Carolina, Tennessee, Texas, and Virginia.

- The Western Association of Schools and Colleges (www.wascweb.org), which covers California, Guam, Hawaii, and U.S. Pacific island territories.

A very small number of online or correspondence schools that lack regional accreditation hold accreditation through a legitimate national accrediting agency, such as the Distance Education and Training Council (DETC), but many diploma mills also operate so-called "accrediting agencies" that offer worthless accreditation so that their worthless degrees sound less worthless. As a general rule, if you're dealing with a U.S. institution, regional accreditation through one of the six agencies listed previously is best. Even legitimate national accrediting bodies like the DETC can't offer the same level of universal recognition. If you're interested in a U.S. school that holds accreditation not specifically mentioned here, make sure the accrediting agency is at least approved by the Council for Higher Education Accreditation (www.chea.org).

Assessing the accreditation status of non-U.S. schools can be difficult. All the non-U.S. schools listed in this appendix are public, state-run universities in their respective nations (Australia, India, South Africa, and the UK) and offer credentials that are internationally recognized as meeting generally accepted accrediting principles. The University of London's External Programme, for example, is a college of England's publicly funded University of London, which has been operating under a royal charter since 1836. As long as you're dealing with a country with a stable, respected educational system, a state-run university is almost certain to be legitimate, for obvious reasons.

Finishing Your Bachelor's Degree: Traditional Online Programs

If you're looking for more of a traditional structure and look forward to taking a series of online courses from the same institution, no worries. All the schools that follow are *somewhat* flexible in their degree requirements (allowing large amounts of transfer credit in most cases, and usually allowing some alternative credit sources), but they're not credit bank programs because all of them require you to take at least some courses from the school you're graduating from.

California State University—Chico

Residency: None required.

Located in: Chico, California

Website: http://rce.csuchico.edu

Relevant degree program: Bachelor of Arts (B.A.) in social science

Central Michigan University

Residency: None required.

Located in: Mount Pleasant, Michigan

Website: www.cel.cmich.edu/ecampus

Relevant degree programs: Bachelor of Science (B.S.) in community development; B.S. in administration, with emphasis in organization administration.

Note: The community development program is available with optional concentrations in community services, health sciences, and public administration.

Colorado State University

Residency: None required.

Located in: Greenwood Village, Colorado

Website: www.csuglobal.org

Relevant degree programs: Bachelor of Arts (B.A.) or Bachelor of Science (B.S.) in applied social sciences; B.S. in organizational leadership.

Note: "Check back with us often," Colorado State's online campus website tells us, "as we will continue offering new, high-demand degrees that reflect the skills needed in the current and always-changing workplace."

WHAT'S IN A MAJOR?

While I list "relevant programs," even at the bachelor's level, most people aren't likely to expect you to have a specialized bachelor's degree in an activism-related field. If the B.S. in management offered by a school looks more up your alley than the B.S. in organizational leadership, you'd probably be as well off with the B.S. in management. Majors become much more important at the graduate level, where *all* coursework is typically in the major field.

Nearly every school I've listed here has degrees other than in the fields listed, so if a particular school looks to be of interest to you but the programs I've described aren't, check out the school's website for other, less-activism-focused program offerings.

Eastern Oregon University

Residency: None required.

Located in: La Grande, Oregon

Website: www.eou.edu

Relevant degree programs: Bachelor of Arts (B.A.) or Bachelor of Science (B.S.) in liberal studies, with emphasis in environmental studies, gender studies, gerontology, Native American studies, or political science; interdisciplinary Bachelor of Arts (B.A.) in philosophy, politics, and economics, with optional concentration in public policy and administration.

Note: An unusually high proportion of EOU's programs seem to be designed with activists in mind.

Empire State College (SUNY)

Residency: None required.

Located in: Saratoga Springs, New York

Website: www.esc.edu

Relevant degree programs: Bachelor of Arts (B.A.) or Bachelor of Science (B.S.) in social theory, social structure and change, with optional concentrations in African American studies, political science, public policy, social theory, sociology, or women's studies; individualized B.A. or B.S. degree.

> > > **N O T E**

"Graduates with a degree in [social theory, social structure, and change] work in a range of social service agencies, social ministry, policy arenas or go on to higher education in the social sciences or social work," the website states.

Florida State University

Residency: None required.

Located in: Tallahassee, Florida

Website: learningforlife.fsu.edu

Relevant degree program: Bachelor of Science (B.S.) in interdisciplinary social science.

Note: This program is intended for students who already hold an associate's degree or the equivalent.

Fort Hays State University

Residency: None required.

Located in: Hays, Kansas

Website: www.fhsu.edu/virtualcollege

Relevant degree programs: Bachelor of Arts (B.A.) in political science; Bachelor of Science (B.S.) in organizational leadership.

Note: FHSU is generally regarded as one of the less expensive distance learning bachelor's programs.

Kansas State University

Residency: None required.

Located in: Manhattan, Kansas

Website: www.dce.k-state.edu

Relevant degree programs: Bachelor of Science (B.S.) in family studies and human services; B.S. in interdisciplinary social science; individualized Bachelor of General Studies (B.G.S.).

Note: The B.S. in family studies and human services generally incorporates an interdisciplinary minor in another field of the student's choice, such as psychology or sociology.

Ohio University

Residency: None required.

Located in: Athens, Ohio

Website: www.ohio.edu/independent

Relevant degree programs: Individualized Bachelor of Specialized Studies (B.S.S.).

Note: The degree is oddly titled, but very flexible. Sample proposals are available on the website for B.S.S. degrees in behavioral studies, conflict and dispute resolution, environmental sciences, family dynamics, gender studies, legal studies, political science and philosophy, social services, women's studies, and youth services. The B.S.S. is intended for students who already hold an associate's degree or the equivalent.

Pennsylvania State University

Residency: None required.

Located in: University Park, Pennsylvania

Website: www.worldcampus.psu.edu

Relevant degree programs: Bachelor of Arts (B.A.) in law and society; Bachelor of Science (B.S.) in organizational leadership.

Note: Penn State has been doing distance learning for more than a century and is surprisingly affordable for such a prestigious school.

Full disclosure: I took Creative Writing 050 by correspondence from Penn State in the early 1990s. (I enjoyed it and finished the course with an A. And yes, I'm bragging.)

University of Maryland—University College

Residency: None required.

Located in: Adelphi, Maryland

Website: www.umuc.edu

Relevant degree programs: Bachelor of Science (B.S.) in legal studies, political science, or social science.

Note: The legal studies program is available with optional minors in criminal justice and political science, and the social science program is available with an optional minor in environmental management.

University of Wisconsin—Superior

Residency: None required.

Located in: Superior, Wisconsin

Website: distancelearning.wisconsin.edu

Relevant degree programs: Bachelor of Arts (B.A.) in organizational administration; Bachelor of Liberal Studies (B.L.S.) in organizational administration; individualized B.A. in interdisciplinary studies; individualized Bachelor of Science (B.S.) program.

Note: The individualized B.S. can be more focused than the individualized B.A., which is more of a liberal arts degree.

Washington State University

Residency: None required.

Located in: Pullman, Washington

Website: online.wsu.edu

Relevant degree programs: Bachelor of Science (B.S.) in social sciences and women's studies.

Note: The social sciences major offers optional concentrations in criminal justice, economics, human development, political science, and women's studies, among other fields.

Master's Programs in Activism-Related Fields

Undergraduate programs in activism are more about getting a degree than actually studying activism—but when you hit the graduate level, you have the opportunity to really specialize in your field of interest.

Antioch University, New England

Residency: None required.

Located in: Keene, New Hampshire

Website: advocacy.antiochne.edu

Relevant degree program: Master of Science (M.S.) in public interest advocacy and organizing.

Note: This is a new program, so details of the curriculum are still being worked out, but there is reason to suspect that specialization tracks will be available.

Athabasca University

Residency: None required.

Located in: Athabasca, Alberta (Canada)

Website: www.athabascau.ca

Relevant degree programs: Master of Arts (M.A.) in integrated studies with optional concentrations in community studies, cultural studies, global change, equity studies, and work, organization, and leadership.

> > > **NOTE**

Athabasca is Canada's answer to the Open University UK or the University of South Africa—a state-run university specifically created to address the needs of distance learners. It has long been a pioneer in online education.

Choose Your Own Academic Adventure

Not satisfied with any of the programs listed here? Antioch University (www.antioch.edu), Goddard College (www.goddard.edu), Lesley University (www.lesley.edu), and National Technological University (www.ntu.edu) all allow students to design individualized low-residency master's programs in consultation with faculty, and the Union Institute and University (www.myunion.edu) has individualized low-residency programs at both the master's and doctoral levels.

Duquesne University

Residency: None required.

Located in: Pittsburgh, Pennsylvania

Website: www.distancelearning.duq.edu

Relevant degree program: Master of Science (M.S.) in community leadership.

Note: According to Duquesne, the program is designed for "the education of leaders who are committed to improving the quality of life within the community," engendering "[a]n understanding of governance, salient community needs and the gap that exists between them."

Empire State College

Residency: Varies by program and may be negotiable.

Located in: Saratoga Springs, New York

Website: www.esc.edu

Relevant degree programs: Master of Arts (M.A.) in labor and policy studies or social policy.

Harvard University

Residency: None required.

Located in: Cambridge, Massachusetts

Website: www.extension.harvard.edu

Relevant degree program: Master of Liberal Arts (M.L.A.) in government or legal studies.

Note: Yes, it's really Harvard.

James Cook University

Residency: None required.

Located in: Townsville, Queensland (Australia)

Website: www.jcu.edu.au

Relevant degree programs: Master of Social Policy; Master of Social Work; Master of Women's Studies.

Note: Postgraduate certificates are also available in the preceding fields.

Kansas State University

Residency: None required.

Located in: Manhattan, Kansas

Website: www.gpidea.org

Relevant degree program: Master of Science (M.S.) in community development.

Note: Concentrations are available in building economic capacity, natural resource management, nonprofit leadership, and working with native communities.

Madurai Kamaraj University

Residency: Exams are typically taken at study centers throughout India, but it is likely that international students can negotiate with MKU to have the exams proctored elsewhere with permission.

Located in: Madurai, Tamil Nadu (India)

Website: www.mkudde.org

Relevant degree programs: Master of Arts (M.A.) in Gandhian thought; M.A. in political science.

Note: Programs are available in both English and Tamil.

Open University UK

Residency: None.

Located in: Milton Keynes, England (United Kingdom)

Website: www.open.ac.uk

Relevant degree programs: Master of Arts (M.A.) in environment, policy, and society; M.A. in social policy and criminology.

Note: An M.A. in social sciences is also available. The Open University is one of the world's largest and most reputable distance-learning-focused institutions.

Oxford University

Residency: One 5-week residency and one 4-week residency, for a total of 9 weeks of residency over the duration of the program.

Located in: Oxford, England (United Kingdom)

Website: humanrightslaw.conted.ox.ac.uk

Relevant degree program: Master of Studies (M.St.) in international human rights law.

Note: Yes, it's really Oxford.

Pennsylvania State University

Residency: None required.

Located in: University Park, Pennsylvania

Website: www.worldcampus.psu.edu

Relevant degree program: Master of Professional Studies (M.P.S.) in community and economic development.

Note: The program is administered under Penn State's agriculture department, which focuses on rural development issues. The program is not irrelevant to urban community and economic development but may be of particular interest to students who want to focus on rural communities.

Pfeiffer University

Residency: None required.

Located in: Charlotte, North Carolina

Website: www.pfeiffer.edu

Relevant degree program: Master of Science (M.S.) in leadership and organizational change.

Note: The program concludes with an applied field project, which can be done locally.

University of Leicester

Residency: None required.

Located in: Leicester, England (United Kingdom)

Website: www.le.ac.uk

Relevant degree programs: Master of Arts (M.A.) in new media, governance, and democracy; Master of Science (M.Sc.) in community safety.

Note: Leicester has been a pioneer in adapting traditional programs to a distance-learning model.

University of London, External System

Residency: None required.

Located in: London, England (United Kingdom)

Website: www.londonexternal.ac.uk

Relevant degree programs: Master of Arts (M.A.) in citizenship education; Master of Research (M.Res.) in educational and social research; Master of Science (M.Sc.) in environmental management; M.Sc. in organizational psychology; M.Sc. in poverty reduction; M.Sc. in public health; M.Sc. in public policy and management.

Note: Formerly known as the University of London External Programme, this is one of the oldest distance learning providers in the world. It is a branch of the University of London, founded in 1836, and programs are created in cooperation with residential colleges (such as the prestigious London School of Economics).

University of Maryland University College

Residency: None required.

Located in: Adelphi, Maryland

Website: www.umuc.edu

Relevant degree program: Master of Science (M.S.) in management, with emphasis in nonprofit management.

Note: "Students entering this program," the description states, "are not required to have backgrounds in any particular educational or professional field."

University of New England

Residency: None required.

Located in: Armidale, New South Wales (Australia)

Website: www.une.edu.au

Relevant degree programs: Master of Arts (M.A.) in peace studies, political and international studies, public policy, regional change management, or women's and gender studies; Master of Professional Studies (M.P.S.) in global futures, migration, and cultures; M.P.S.

in peace studies; Master of Environmental Systems, Markets, and Climate Change; Master of Organizational Development and Strategic Human Resource Management.

Note: This school, one of the largest public universities in Australia, should not be confused with University of New England in Maine.

University of South Africa

Residency: None required.

Located in: Johannesburg, Gauteng (South Africa)

Website: www.unisa.ac.za

Relevant degree programs: Master of Arts (M.A.) in African politics, development studies, environmental management, industrial and organizational psychology, international politics, politics, and social science; Master of Theology (Th.M.) in missiology, with emphasis in urban ministry.

Note: UNISA is one of the largest distance education institutions in the world and boasts Nelson Mandela and Desmond Tutu among its graduates.

Traditional Doctoral Programs in Activism-Related Fields

Yes, you can actually get a doctorate online. Most of these programs require *some* time on campus (whereas most of the bachelor's and master's programs listed in this appendix do not), but not very much.

Antioch University

Residency: One weeklong residency in Ohio every summer and three weekend residencies held throughout the year at sites on the west coast and New England.

Located in: Yellow Springs, Ohio

Website: www.phd.antioch.edu

Relevant degree program: Doctor of Philosophy (Ph.D.) in leadership and organizational change.

Capella University

Residency: Three 5-day residencies over the course of the program.

Located in: Minneapolis, Minnesota

Website: www.capella.edu

Relevant degree programs: Doctor of Philosophy (Ph.D.) in human services, with optional specialization tracks in management of nonprofit agencies and social/community services; Ph.D. in organization and management.

University of Phoenix

Residency: A total of 16 days of residency at various seminars that are held at locations throughout the country, spread out over three years.

Located in: Phoenix, Arizona

Website: www.phoenix.edu

Relevant degree program: Doctor of Management (D.Mgmt.) in organizational leadership.

University of South Africa

Residency: None required.

Located in: Johannesburg, Gauteng (South Africa)

Website: www.unisa.ac.za

Relevant degree programs: Doctor of Literature and Philosophy (D.Litt. et Phil.) in development studies, environmental management, industrial and organizational psychology, politics, or public administration; Doctor of Philosophy (D.Phil.) in development studies or environmental management; Doctor of Theology (D.Th.) in missiology, with emphasis in urban ministries.

Note: UNISA is one of the largest distance education institutions in the world and boasts Nelson Mandela and Desmond Tutu among its graduates.

Walden University

Residency: Twenty days over the course of the program, divided into two 4-day residencies and two 6-day residencies.

Located in: Minneapolis, Minnesota

Website: www.waldenu.edu

Relevant degree programs: Doctor of Philosophy (Ph.D.) in human services; Ph.D. in public policy and administration, with optional specialization tracks in international nongovernmental organizations (NGOs), law and public policy, nonprofit management and leadership, local government management for sustainable community, and public policy.

Note: Has no relationship with the fictional Walden University from *Doonesbury*.

Negotiable Research Doctorates

In Britain, Australia, South Africa, and other Commonwealth countries, the Ph.D. typically involves no coursework in the area of study but consists entirely of a dissertation. For obvious reasons, this means a great deal of flexibility in what can be done online versus what can be done in person.

Most of these schools have minimum residency requirements, but even for some of the most prestigious universities, residency for a research doctorate can be as minimal as one weekend per year. If there's an institution not on this list that appeals to you, and it's in the former British Commonwealth, check with the school to see if you can do the doctorate off campus as an international student.

Index

Numerics

52 Ways to Change the World! with Julie Zauzmer podcast, 84

501c organizations, 69

2006 Day Without Protests, as online multimedia activism tool, 80

2007 Burmese protests, online multimedia example, 76–77

2009 Iranian protests, online multimedia example, 75–76

A

Absolute Beginner's Guide to Computer Basics (5th edition, Que Publishing, 2009), 7

Abu Ghraib, online multimedia activism example, 77

accreditation

　bachelor's degree activism programs, 169–170

　diploma mills, 170

ACLU (American Civil Liberties Union) Twitter feed, 77

　adoption of online activism, 8–10

　Twitter feed, 93

action alerts

　action items, writing, 107–108

　alerts, writing, 104–107

activism, 61–62

　careers, 133–135

　degree programs

　　associate's degrees, 168

　　bachelor's degrees, 168–174

　　doctoral programs, 179–180

　　master's degrees, 174–179

　online mistakes, avoiding

　　attention-starved users (chats), 130

　　blogosphere flamewars, 128

　　forwarding unsourced chain letters, 128

　　installing social networking applications, 130

　　interpersonal politics, 129–130

　　multitasking, 131

　　reading/writing vitriol (anger), 129

　　self-promotion, 130

　　sloth/procrastination, 131–132

　　unproductive online debate-oriented issue groups, 129

Adams, John, 116, 147

adoption of online activism by traditional activist groups, 8–10

Ahmadinejad, Mahmoud, 75

Alinsky, Saul, 10, 51–53, 89

Allen, George, campaign video as multimedia activism tool, 79

Amanpour: The Power of the Interview podcast, 85

Amnesty International Twitter feed, 93

anger (vitriol), reading/writing, 129

answering email messages, 91

Anti-Saloon League, 117

Antikythera mechanism, 143

Antioch University, 174–175, 179

Apple II, 153

applications (social networking), installing, 130

ARC (Archival Research Catalog), finding photographs online, 83

ARPANET, 152

artisans' strike, 141

Ashoka, 142

associate's degree activism programs, 168

Athabasca University, 175

attention-starved users (chats), 130

audience, finding for websites
cross-links, 39
nonlocal supporters, 29–30
ColorOfChange.org case study, 30–35
donations, 32–34
media relations, 36–37
organizing local supporters, 24
Coalition on Homelessness, San Francisco case study, 24–25, 28
controlling local messages via main page, 25–26

fact sheets, 28–29
local meetings, 27–28
multiple languages, 26
organization's physical address, 26
reports, 28–29
talking points, 28–29
print media, 40
repeat visitors, 39
search engines, 38–39
social networking websites, 39
word of mouth, 40

audio, podcasting, 83–87

Aung San Suu Kyi, 76

Ayatollah Khamenei, 75

B

Babylonian captivity, preservation of Jewish scriptures during, 141

Babylonian Talmud, 144

bachelor's degree activism programs, 168
accreditation, 169–170
diploma mills, 170
online programs, 171–174

Bachmann, Michelle, 58

BBC documentary podcasts, 86

BBS (bulletin board system), 153–154
social networking, development of, 43–44

Bell, Alexander Graham, 149–150

Berners Lee, Tim, 155

Big Vision with Britt Bravo podcast, 86

Bill Moyers: Journal podcast, 85

Bioneers podcast, 84

blogging, 98–101

bloggingheads.tv podcast, 86

blogs
flamewars, 128
vitriol (anger), reading/writing, 129

Blogspot, 99

Borrmann, Martin, 167

Boyd, Krys, 87

Bravo, Britt, 86

Brevísima Relación de la Destrucción de las Indias (de las Casas), 146

Buck, James Karl, 96

bulk SMS messaging, 96

bulletin board system (BBS), 153–154

Burmese protest of 2007, multimedia as activism tool, 76–77

Bush, George H.W., 121

C

CafePress, 68

California State University-Chico, 171

Capella University, 179

careers
in activism, 133–135
job searching, 137

Carlson, Bruce, 86

Case Foundation Twitter feed, 95

Cato Weekly Video podcast, 85

cave paintings, 139–140

cell phones, invention of, 151–152

Central Michigan University, 171

chain letters, forwarding, 128

Change.org Twitter feed, 93

CharityAdvantage, 70

Charter Oak State College, 168

chats, attention-starved users, 130

Chauvet-Pont-d'Arc Cave, 73

checks, processing online donations, 69
Chideya, Farai, 93
Civil War, telegraph in, 148–149
Clinton, Bill, 10, 110
Coalition on Homelessness, website development case study, 24–25, 28
collaborative documents, effect on activism, 122
Colorado State University, 171
ColorLines Twitter feed, 95
ColorOfChange.org, 30–35, 64
comments in blogs, 99
Common Sense (1776), 115, 147
communicants, 90
communication with supporters, 89–90
   answering email messages, 91
   blogging, 98–101
   bulk SMS messaging, 96
   importance of, 101
   newsletters, 91–93
   Twitter, 93–98
Community Memory, 153
CommunityConnect social networking website, 49
CompuServe, 154
computers
   Antikythera mechanism, 143
   ARPANET, 152
   Community Memory, 153
   CompuServe, 154
   dialup BBS, 153–154
   ENIAC, 150
   Facebook, 155–156
   FidoNet, 154
   integrated circuits, 151
   personal computers, 153

Project Gutenberg, 152–153
   World Wide Web, 155
concerned citizens as online activists, 123–124
Constant Contact, creating newsletters, 92
counterfeit activism, 108
creating podcasts, 84
Creative Commons, finding photographs online, 83
credit bank programs, bachelor's degree activism programs, 168
   accreditation, 169–170
   diploma mills, 170
credit cards, processing online donations, 69
cross-links, bringing traffic to websites, 39

D

DailyKos, 100, 156
dailymotion.com, uploading video, 81
Day Without Immigrants protests, as online multimedia activism tool, 80
de las Casas, Bartolomé, 146
debate-oriented issue groups, avoiding unproductive groups, 129
decisionmakers, selecting, 105
degree programs in activism
   associate's degrees, 168
   bachelor's degrees, 168–169
      accreditation, 169–170
      diploma mills, 170
      online programs, 171–174
   doctoral programs, 179–180
   master's degrees, 174–179

Delany, Colin, 63
Democracy Now! with Amy Goodman podcast, 85
DETC (Distance Education and Training Council), activism degree program accreditation, 170
dialup BBS, 153–154
diploma mills, bachelor's degree program accreditation, 170
distance learning, online fundraising, 68
doctoral activism programs, 179–180
donations
   online processing, 69–70
   soliciting, 32–34
Duquesne University, 175

E

Eastern Oregon University, 172
eBooks, 152–153
educational programs, online fundraising, 68
EFF (Electronic Frontier Foundation), 110
effectiveness of petitions, 109–111
email
   action alerts, writing, 104–108
   messages, answering, 91
   newsletters, writing, 91–93
Empire State College (SUNY), 172, 176
encyclical letters, 143–144
ENIAC (Electronic Numerical Indicator and Computer), 150
Ensler, Eve, 84
EQCA (Equality California), media relations and websites, 37

ethics of activism, 61–62
Ethos Roundtable, 6
evolving technologies effecting activism
    collaborative documents, 122
    mobile access, 122
    security, 123
    Web 2.0, 122
Excelsior College, 169

F

Facebook, 46, 155–156
    Obama campaign case study, 46
    traffic, bringing to websites, 39
fact sheets, organizing via supporters, 28–29
Fareed Zakaria: GPS podcast, 85
feeds (Twitter), list of, 93–95
Feminist Career Center, 138
Feminist Majority Foundation Twitter feed, 93
FidoNet, 154
finding photographs online, 82–83
Fine, Allison, 86
Five Good Things in the World podcast, 84
flamewars, blogs and, 128
Flannery, Matt, 71
Flickr
    finding photographs online, 83
    posting photographs online, 82
Florida State University, 172
Fort Hays State University, 172–173
Forum with Michael Krasny podcast, 86
forwarding unsourced chain letters, 128
friends, social networking, 45

Friendster, 49, 155
fundraising, online, 63–70

G

Gandhi, Mahatma, 52
Garrison, William Lloyd, 116
genocide in New World, 146–147
Gilfillan, S.C., 119
Goddard College, 175
Goodman, Amy, 85
Google Wave service, 122
Grameen Bank, 70–71
grant funding, 66–67
Grant, Oscar, shooting video as multimedia activism tool, 78
grants.gov, 66
graphics in newsletters, 92
groups (social networking), 45
Gutenberg, Johannes, 115
Guttmacher Institute Twitter feed, 93

H

hacktivism, 55–57
Hagia Sophia, 145
Hart, Michael, 152
Harvard University, 176
Hebrew Bible, preservation of, 141
Henry, Patrick, 62
history of online activism
    Antikythera mechanism, 143
    ARPANET, 152
    Ashoka's pillars, 142
    Babylonian captivity, preservation of Jewish scriptures, 141
    Babylonian Talmud, 144
    cave paintings, 139–140
    cell phones, 151–152
    Common Sense (1776), 147

Community Memory, 153
CompuServe, 154
dialup BBS, 153–154
ENIAC, 150
epistle to the Thessalonians, 143–144
Facebook, 155–156
FidoNet, 154
genocide in New World, 146–147
Hagia Sophia, 145
House of Wisdom in Baghdad, 145–146
integrated circuits, 151
Kennedy-Nixon debate, 151
Medinet Habu artisans' strike, 141
personal computers, 153
praise poem of Urukagina, 140–141
Project Gutenberg, 152–153
telegraph, 148–149
telephone, 149–150
Uncle Tom's Cabin (Stowe), 148
world wide web, 155
Hitchens, Christopher, 58
House of Wisdom in Baghdad, 145–146
HTML newsletters, plain text newsletters versus, 92

I

IBM PC, 153
IBM PCjr, 153
iContact newsletters, creating, 91
Idealist.org, 49, 84, 137
Ifill, Gwen, 85
The Influence of Invention and Discovery, Vol 1, 119
integrated circuits, 151
intermediary services, processing online donations, 70

Internet
  ARPANET, 152
  CompuServe, 154
  Facebook, 155–156
  need for online
    presence, 6
  World Wide Web, 155
interpersonal politics,
  avoiding, 129–130
Iranian protests of 2009,
  multimedia as activism
  tool, 75–76
issue groups, avoiding
  unproductive debate-
  oriented groups, 129
issues, researching
  blogs, 19–21
  laws and legislation,
    18–19
  news sites, 19
  print publications, 17
  resources, 15–17

J

Jackley, Jessica, 71
Jacobs, Harriet, 116
James Cook
University, 176
Jennings, Tom, 154
Jewish scriptures,
preservation of, 141
job searching, 137
Jones, Van, 84
JustGive, 70

K

Kansas State University,
173, 176
Kennedy, John F., 120
Kennedy-Nixon
debate, 121, 151
Kilby, Jack, 151
Kim, Catherine, 9
Kiva, 71
Krasny, Michael, 86
Kristof, Nicholas, 95

L

Leopold's Records, 43, 153
Lesley University, 175
Lewis, C.S, 7
Library of Congress, finding
photographs online, 83
Lincoln, Abraham, 148–149
LinkedIn social networking
website, 49
links
  cross-links, bringing traf-
    fic to websites, 39
  in Twitter tweets, 98
livevideo.com, uploading
video, 81
loans, Grameen Bank, 70–71
local support, organizing
(website development), 24
  Coalition on
    Homelessness, San
    Francisco case study,
    24–25, 28
  fact sheets, 28–29
  local meetings, 25–28
  multiple languages, 26
  organization's physical
    address, 26
  reports, 28–29
  talking points, 28–29
Lovejoy, Elijah P., 116

M

Macintosh, 153
Madoff, Bernie, 87
Madurai Kamaraj
University, 176
main page (websites),
organizing via local
supporters, 25–26
Mam, Somaly, 95
Maree, Mohammed, 96
Martin, Michel, 86
Mashable Twitter feed, 94
mass media,
monuments as, 142

master's degree activism
programs, 174–179
Matson, Erin, 93
McClellan, George, 148
McLuhan, Marshall, 139
media relations, websites
and
  EQCA case study, 37
  NOW case study, 36
Medinet Habu artisans'
strike, 141
meetings (local), organizing
via supporters, 27–28
Mehserle, Joe, 78
memberships, online
fundraising, 68
merchandising, online
fundraising, 68
Middle States Association of
Colleges and Schools,
activism degree program
accreditation, 170
Mikkelson, Barbara, 108
Miller, Michael, 7
mistakes in online activism,
avoiding
  attention-starved users
    (chats), 130
  blogosphere
    flamewars, 128
  interpersonal politics,
    129–130
  multitasking, 131
  reading/writing vitriol
    (anger), 129
  self-promotion, 130
  sloth/procrastination,
    131–132
  social networking
    applications,
    installing, 130
  unproductive online
    debate-oriented issue
    groups, 129
  unsourced chain letters,
    forwarding, 128

mobile access, effect on activism, 122
mobile phones, 151
money orders, processing online donations, 69
monuments as mass media, 142
Mother Jones Podcast, 86
MoveOn.org, 10, 65
Moyers, Bill, 85
multimedia
    as activism tool
        2006 Day Without Immigrants protests, 80
        2007 Burmese protests, 76–77
        2009 Iranian protests, 75–76
        Abu Ghraib, 77
        George Allen campaign video, 79
        shooting video of Oscar Grant, 78
    photographs
        finding online, 82–83
        posting online, 82
    podcasting, 83–87
    video
        online streaming, 81
        uploading to websites, 80–81
multitasking, excessive, 131
My History Can Beat Up Your Politics podcast, 86
MySpace, 39, 48, 155

N

NAACP Twitter feed, 94
National Council of La Raza website, 66
National Organization for Women (NOW) Twitter feed, 93
National Technological University, 175

NetworkForGood, 70, 94
New England Association of Schools and Colleges, activism degree program accreditation, 170
New World, genocide in, 146–147
newsletters, writing, 91–93
Nielsen, Jakob, 92
Ning social networking website, 48
Nixon, Richard, 120
Nixon-Kennedy debate, 151
nonlocal support, organizing (website development), 29–30
    ColorOfChange.org case study, 30–35
    donations, 32–34
    media relations
        EQCA case study, 37
        NOW case study, 36
nonprofit organizations, online memberships
    distance learning, 68
    fundraising, 68
Nonprofit Oyster, 137
North Central Association of Colleges and Schools, activism degree program accreditation, 170
Northwest Association of Accredited Schools, activism degree program accreditation, 170
NOW (National Organization for Women)
    media relations and websites, 36
    Twitter feed, 93
NRA (National Rifle Association), 6

O

O'Brien, Michael, 120
Obama, Barack, Facebook

social networking case study, 46
Ogburn, W.F., 119
Ohio University, 173
online activism, 7
    history of
        Antikythera mechanism, 143
        ARPANET, 152
        Ashoka's pillars, 142
        Babylonian captivity, preservation of Jewish scriptures, 141
        Babylonian Talmud, 144
        cave paintings, 139–140
        cell phones, 151–152
        Common Sense (1776), 147
        Community Memory, 153
        CompuServe, 154
        dialup BBS, 153–154
        ENIAC, 150
        epistle to the Thessalonians, 143–144
        Facebook, 155–156
        FidoNet, 154
        genocide in New World, 146–147
        Hagia Sophia, 145
        House of Wisdom in Baghdad, 145–146
        integrated circuits, 151
        Kennedy-Nixon debate, 151
        Medinet Habu artisans' strike, 141
        personal computers, 153
        praise poem of Urukagina, 140–141
        Project Gutenberg, 152–153

telegraph, 148–149
telephone, 149–150
Uncle Tom's Cabin
(Stowe), 148
World Wide Web, 155
mistakes, avoiding
attention-starved users
(chats), 130
blogosphere flame-
wars, 128
interpersonal politics,
129–130
multitasking, 131
online debate-oriented
issue groups, 129
reading/writing vitriol
(anger), 129
self-promotion, 130
sloth/procrastination,
131–132
social networking
applications,
installing, 130
unsourced chain let-
ters, forwarding, 128
MoveOn.org, 10
petitions, 108–111
seven deadly sins
being scary, 59, 61
hacktivism, 55–57
nagging, 57–58
self-promotion at the
expense of the move-
ment, 53–54
unsolicited bulk mail,
54–55
violating copyright, 57
violating privacy,
58–59
online activists
concerned citizens,
123–124
outreachers, 125–126
professional, 124–125
online donation
processing, 69–70

online fundraising, 63–64,
66–67
donations, processing,
69–70
through distance
learning, 68
through
memberships, 68
through
merchandising, 68
online multimedia
as activism tool
2006 Day Without
Immigrants
protests, 80
2007 Burmese protests,
76–77
2009 Iranian protests,
75–76
Abu Ghraib, 77
George Allen cam-
paign video, 79
shooting video of
Oscar Grant, 78
photographs
finding online, 82–83
posting online, 82
podcasting, 83–87
video
streaming, 81
uploading to websites,
80–81
online presence, need for, 6
Open University UK, 175–177
Opportunity Knocks, 137
Orkut social networking
website, 49
outreachers as online
activists, 125–126
Oxford University, 177

P-Q

Paine, Thomas, 115, 147
Paul of Tarsus, 143–144
PayPal, processing online
donations, 70

Pennsylvania State
University, 173, 177
personal computers, history
of, 153
petitions, 108–111
Pfeiffer University, 177
PFLAG (Parents, Friends and
Families of Lesbians and
Gays) website, 65
Ph.D activism programs,
179–180
photographs
finding online, 82–83
posting online, 82
plain text newsletters, HTML
newsletters versus, 92
podcasts, 83–87
52 Ways to Change the
World! with Julie
Zauzmer podcast, 84
Amanpour: The Power of
the Interview podcast, 85
BBC documentary pod-
casts, 86
Big Vision with Britt Bravo
podcast, 86
Bill Moyers: Journal
podcast, 85
Bioneers podcast, 84
bloggingheads.tv
podcast, 86
Cato Weekly Video
podcast, 85
Democracy Now! with
Amy Goodman
podcast, 85
Fareed Zakaria: GPS
podcast, 85
Five Good Things in the
World podcast, 84
Forum with Michael
Krasny podcast, 86
Mother Jones
Podcast, 86
My History Can Beat Up
Your Politics podcast, 86

Social Good with Allison Fine podcast, 86
Tell Me More podcast, 86
Washington Post podcasts, 85
Washington Week with Gwen Ifill podcast, 85
posting photographs online, 82
praise poem of Urukagina, 140–141
Prejean, Helen, 94
preservation of Jewish scriptures, 141
print media, bringing traffic to websites, 40
printing press, effect on activism, 115–117
processing online donations, 69–70
procrastination/sloth, online activism, 131–132
professional online activists, 124–125
profiles (social networking), 44
Project Gutenberg, 152–153
publicity, 89

R

radio, effect on activism, 118–119
raising money. *See* online fundraising
Rameses III, 141
Rav Ashi, 144
Reagan, Ronald, 119
Reason Twitter feed, 95
Recent Social Trends in the United States, 118
Reiter, Lea, 94
repeat visitors, bringing traffic to websites, 39
reports, organizing via supporters, 28–29

researching issues, 21
blogs, 19, 21
laws and legislation, 18–19
news sites, 19
print publications, 17
resources, 15–17
Roman Empire, Hagia Sophia, 145
Roosevelt, Franklin D., 119
Rules For Radicals (1971), 10, 51

S

Saratovsky, Kari, 95
Schlotzer, Alex, 122
search engines, bringing traffic to websites, 38–39
searching for jobs in activism, 137
security, effect on activism, 123
Segal, Meredith, Obama campaign case study, 47
selecting decisionmakers, 105
self-promotion, excessiveness, 130
seven deadly sins of online activism
    being scary, 59–61
    hacktivism, 55–57
    nagging, 57–58
    self-promotion at the expense of the movement, 53–54
    unsolicited bulk mail, 54–55
    violating copyright, 57
    violating privacy, 58–59
Sidarth, S.R., 79
SisterSong Twitter feed, 95
sloth/procrastination, avoiding, 131–132
Smith, Jamil, 94
SMS messaging, 69, 96
snopes.com, 108

Social Edge Twitter feed, 95
Social Good with Allison Fine podcast, 86
social networking, 50, 155–156
    applications, installing, 130
    CommunityConnect, 49
    development of, 43–44
    Facebook, 46
    friends, 45
    Friendster, 49
    groups, 45
    Idealist.org, 49
    LinkedIn, 49
    MySpace, 48
    Ning, 48
    Orkut, 49
    problems with, 45
    profiles, 44
    Twitter, 49
    websites, bringing traffic to, 39
soliciting donations, websites, 32–34
Southern Association of Colleges and Schools, activism degree program accreditation, 170
staying informed, methods of, 21
    blogs, 19–21
    laws and legislation, 18–19
    news sites, 19
    print publications, 17
    resources, 15–17
Stevenson, Adlai, 120
Stokowski, Leopold, 43
Stowe, Harriett Beecher, 148
streaming video online, 81
subscribers for newsletters, 92
SUNY (Empire State College), 172

supporters, communication with, 89–90
    answering email message, 91
    blogging, 98–101
    bulk SMS messaging, 96
    importance of, 101
    newsletters, 91–93
    Twitter, 93–98

T

Tactical Technology Collective Twitter feed, 94
talking points, organizing via supporters, 28–29
Talmud, 144
Tandy 1000, 153
technology, effect on activism
    evolving technologies
        collaborative documents, 122
        mobile access, 122
        security, 123
        Web 2.0, 122
    printing press, 115–117
    radio, 118–119
    telegraph, 117
    telephone, 117
    television, 120–121
Technorati, 101
telegraph, 117, 148–149
telephone
    cell phones, invention of, 151–152
    effect on activism, 117
    in history of online activism, 149–150
television
    effect on activism, 120–121
    Kennedy-Nixon debate, 151
Tell Me More podcast, 86
text messaging, 96

The Foundation Center, The website, 66
Thessalonians, epistle to, 143–144
Think with Krys Boyd podcast, 87
Thomas Edison State College, 169
traditional activist organizations adoption of online activism, 8–10
Trippi, Joe, 94
Twitter, 49, 93–98
    frequently asked questions, 97–98
    list of feeds, 93–95
two-year (associates) degree programs, 168

U

Uncle Tom's Cabin (Stowe), 148
UNICEF Twitter feed, 95
Union Institute and University, 175
University of Leicester, 178
University of London's External Programme, 170
University of London, External System, 178
University of Maryland University College, 174, 178
University of New England, 178–179
University of Phoenix, 180
University of South Africa, 175, 179–180
University of Wisconsin-Superior, 174
unproductive debate-oriented issue groups, avoiding, 129
unsourced chain letters, forwarding, 128
uploading video to websites, 80–81

Urukagina, praise poem of, 140–141

V

video
    online streaming, 81
    podcasting, 83–87
    uploading to websites, 80–81
visitors (repeat), bringing traffic to websites, 39
vitriol, reading/writing, 129
Voters Telecommunications Watch, 110

W

Walden University, 180
WANK worm, 55–57
Washington Post podcasts, 85
Washington State University, 174
Washington Week with Gwen Ifill podcast, 85
Web 2.0, 99, 122
web pages, writing action alerts, 104–108
Webb, Jim, 79
websites
    audience, finding
        Coalition on Homelessness, San Francisco case study, 24–25, 28
        controlling local messages via main page, 25–26
        cross-links, 39
        donations, 32–34
        fact sheets, 28–29
        local meetings, 27–28
        media relations, 36–37
        multiple languages, 26
        nonlocal supporters, 29–37
        organization's physical address, 26

organizing local supporters, 24–29
print media, 40
repeat visitors, 39
reports, 28–29
search engines, 38–39
social networking websites, 39
talking points, 28–29
word of mouth, 40
building, keys to, 40
capabilities of, 41–42
online fundraising, 63–67
    through educational programs, 68
    through memberships, 68
    through merchandising, 68
Western Association of Schools and Colleges, activism degree program accreditation, 170
Wikimedia Commons, finding photographs online, 83
Wired Twitter feed, 95
WITNESS Twitter feed, 95
word of mouth, bringing

traffic to websites, 40
WordPress, 99
world wide web, 155
writing action alerts, 104–108

X-Y-Z

Yahoo! Groups, creating newsletters, 91
YouTube, uploading video, 80
Yunus, Muhammad, 70

Zakaria, Fareed, 85
Zarrella, Dan, 97

FREE Online Edition

Your purchase of **It's Your World, So Change It** includes access to a free online edition for 45 days through the Safari Books Online subscription service. Nearly every Que book is available online through Safari Books Online, along with more than 5,000 other technical books and videos from publishers such as Addison-Wesley Professional, Cisco Press, Exam Cram, IBM Press, O'Reilly, Prentice Hall, and Sams.

SAFARI BOOKS ONLINE allows you to search for a specific answer, cut and paste code, download chapters, and stay current with emerging technologies.

Activate your FREE Online Edition at www.informit.com/safarifree

> **STEP 1:** Enter the coupon code: PWEXAZG.

> **STEP 2:** New Safari users, complete the brief registration form.
> Safari subscribers, just log in.

If you have difficulty registering on Safari or accessing the online edition, please e-mail customer-service@safaribooksonline.com